GOD OR SPACE?

What difference does it make?

[rewiring the human perception of time]

Table of Contents

Note from the Author

Some of the issues addressed in this book are not intended to be resolved by examination through the scope of any particular field of study. I wish to differentiate the present work from all formal bodies of knowledge. Meaning, I'm trying to avoid stepping into the particular concepts of specific academic disciplines. Defining concepts pertaining to mathematics, physics, biology – or any other science – is not my purpose in this book.

My intention is to clear the trappings of traditional academia from the reader's path. I'm going to navigate the field of human experience from the view of a "naked human who sees and can talk about what it sees," and who is delving into the experience of observing raw time and space. That is, I'm not seeking any specific domain, but instead to open the door for every possible domain.

In order to simplify the process of writing, I wish to respectfully make a general distinction about the gender pronouns used throughout the work. God is referred to as "he," without the intention to portray God as either man or woman, but rather as both or neither (as the reader chooses). Similarly, the words "human" and "man" imply the whole of the human race.

In the case where etymologies are used, my aim is to shed light on the meaning of certain contexts. Although the general use of a word's etymological root is to show its historical development, here I'm not studying the progress of linguistic structures in any sense. Before any word can actually become a word, it has to have a relationship to a meaning – whether cultural or biological – and it is just that to which I want to expose you. As metaphors, relationships are established through the abstraction of space and time in the human mind, to come out of the body in the form of sounds or shapes. I'll be using references to partially trace the structure of such shapes to depict how we see reality before it becomes words and symbols.

Acknowledgements

With special thanks to:

My parents, my loving wife and children, who are my source of inspiration;

My brother, who encouraged me to follow an artistic life;

All of those who were before us, and out of passion left us invaluable knowledge;

All the living who are putting their content into action through the word and work.

Introduction

This work is the result of humanity's search for truth and change. As living creatures, since time immemorial, our main concern has remained unchanged. Humanity has built great civilizations, developed extraordinary technology, mastered atomic energy, devised artificial intelligence, and succeeded in many more accomplishments that were unthinkable to the ancient people of the world. However, the most profound preoccupation of the modern human is still the same of that of the very first man to ever exist. We die, and there's nothing we can do about it, or that's what we think. Life in general exists because one day it won't. Humanity has been in an infant state with regards to the matter of death right from the beginning.

In this book, the goal is to explore the most basic aspects of human reality, so as to determine what our true condition is, and if there's anything we can do about it. The aim is to embark on this quest without approaching human issues from specific ideas or ideals. In fact, what is proposed is entirely the opposite. I'll delve into what it means to have ideas and to have an ideal, and whether they are related at all to the issue of death. I'll be moving from the most fundamental to the most complex issue in human experience, and you are going to see if the two are really that different.

This work is divided into three parts. The first part is oriented to show you the psychological distortion humans currently experience as a result of the work of time, as we idealize it. Meaning, without a particular direction or methodology, I'm going to expose the problem that time presents in psychological terms in our daily lives. In light of that, I'll seek first to provide you with the necessary insight so that you can see for yourself what reality actually means. The objective is to place yourself in a field common to all humanity. It is out of that common ground that the rest of the meaning of the book will unfold. I will cover what I perceive as space, and what I believe is its function in reality. Then, I will invite the reader to analyze whether physical space is different from psychological space, and what this means for all of us. I'll continue through with the concept of time. Likewise, as I'll do with space, I'll encourage you to observe what time actually is, and if it differs psychologically from physically. Finally, I'll combine the two to construct the foundations for knowledge, and build a psychological layout for the perception of reality.

The second part of the book will target the subject of God. As in the case of part one, I am not going to be discussing historical facts or particular theological frameworks. Following the course of ideas in the previous chapters, the purpose of this section is not to define God or idealize him. Instead, we will seek to understand the relationship of the idea of God with what we call death, and if the idea of God is different from what we understand as space. In this section, I'll also discuss whether God as a purpose in life is possible, and the implications of this for the human condition.

Finally, in part three, I'm going to cover issues about the human condition in general. As you wrap it all up, you'll see how and why humanity gives meaning to life. The need for a savior, and some adult fairy tales, are going to be put to the test. Moreover, I'll discuss the significance of living an artistic life, and what the relationship between that life and happiness is. Additionally, there will be a distinction drawn between art and beauty, and we'll look into the possibility of leading a life that is full of energy. I'll guide you through an evaluation of what the relationship between an ideal and the observer is, and how that determines the relationship between observers themselves. You'll figure as you read whether human relationships can exist without the pursuit of time. I'll explore how the observing of our own sorrow reveals the sorrow of all humanity, and how seeing it changes the mind of the observer.

A creative life is a healthier life. Humans are the best artists on planet Earth; yet, because of the ways of our modern world, we are becoming extremely mechanical beings. I am particularly interested in raising awareness of the dangers of living this way. More than seeing the need for a change, we need to return to basics, to the point in time where all we had in common was our nature. From that space, and using the power of knowledge, we can rebuild our relationships, and lead a more creative existence. With the conviction that we have the spirit of the creator we call God within us, I'm looking forward to encouraging people to live a life freer from modern psychological distortions, and to be more energetic in their doings.

PART 1 **– SPACE: ONE AND UNKNOWN**

Chapter 1

SPACE

THE SEARCH FOR THE UNKNOWN
IS THE MOVEMENT OF THE KNOWN.
SUCH MOTION REMAINS FOREVER UNKNOWN.

There was once a creature, a special one, with a unique spatial ability. This creature was capable of observing the world and separating itself from all other things. It thrived and would give birth to more beings alike, who would later call themselves Humans. Man and woman; that's how they would label their kind, and they would give names to all other things that they saw apart from themselves. These humans would go so far as to label each other at birth with specific names in order to differentiate one from the other. Eventually, man observed the entire existence in a single field, one in which all things have a place, including himself, and he would call that field *The Universe.*

For millennia, humans have conceptualized and defined their greatest evolutionary development as the ability to be conscious. Man is thus convinced he is aware of his own existence. Because of our physical bodies, we are first aware of all external existence, and then psychologically we split from the rest. We are conscious of the fact we "are" only in reference to a coordinate within the field we call the universe — but how are we aware of ourselves? Our relationship with the world is the result of our consciousness functioning; nevertheless, such a function is brought about by a set of relationships. The natural question would be, which one comes first? Is our consciousness an emergent function that's a result of our relationships, or are our relationships the result of our consciousness functioning? We establish relationships via limits. A limitation is presented as one or several sets of coordinates to which we bear a relationship, and that brings about a psychological function. Thus, it seems as if function, or at least motion, comes first. What humanity has questioned from the very beginning is whether that function is what each of us call "*I am?*" I propose that all possible answers to the previous, and to all other existing questions, lie in *Space* itself.

Awareness of the vastness or the narrowness, of that which is in between, is what really makes us humans one of a kind. The notion of space has always been part of human consciousness. In fact, human consciousness exits from space and manifests as part of what we know, which is the domain of time acting in the appearance of everything. Space is as present in the external world as it is in the internal. It is as real as psychological, and it is the powerhouse of the whole of existence. Space is omnipresent, and it somehow seems to be omnipotent as well – an aspect we'll be exploring later on. It doesn't have a nature because it is in itself that which gives birth to all things; everything that exists emerges from t, not the other way around. One could say that God, the creator, lies in space, or that God is space, because it is everywhere and everything comes from it. But, what is space in the first place? Is it definable? Does it have any domain, limits, properties, or function? Can we study it, know it, and therefore be able to dominate it? Could it be possible at all to ever touch it, or to at least grasp it? Is space even a thing? Well, it was just said that it makes all that there is possible, but the depths of its role are much more than that. *Space is itself all possibilities.*

There is no starting point from which to begin enquiring about space because it goes in all directions. It even precedes time, and it will still be there after time. For this reason, in order to follow what is meant here by "space," we must comprehend that there are not different kinds of it. There is not a space that it is somehow filled, and then another space that is completely empty. There is not a type of space on earth that's saturated with molecules and particles, and an outer space that's devoid of all possibility. Across the entire field, at all levels of observation, the space that's present must be absolute. Is there anything to perceive about the void then? Since perception occurs at the limits of the conceivable, what there really is to ever know is a series of limits which exist in a relationship to one another. Space is the pause in between those relationships. The fact that a relationship requires two or more limits sets the reader on the path to an irrevocable truth, which is the perpetual presence of space in between.

Although we can't measure space, it determines the quality of all relationships. We live through images related to one another. Everything in the field of the known is known because every limit in our content is contiguous to the next. Out of this, another important aspect to consider arises; just as there is one type of space, let us say there is only one kind of "image." We are not talking just about visual images. We will consider any given form an image – form being what the senses, or whatever the instrument of perception might be, draw from the distortion of the observed field. Before further expanding on this particular point, let's simplify by stating that whatever is not emptiness is an image. Whatever is not empty can be known, and it bears a form because it is limited. The known has to have at least two limits; a beginning limit and an ending limit. It includes ideas, feelings, thoughts, and all other possible realities. *The known is consciousness' limit, and any limit is time.*

Just as the earth and the moon set their precise place in the universe, and a reader sets the right distance between himself and a book, a writer makes sure there is proper spacing between words and lines, and the mind of the last two establishes a relationship between what is being said and reality. *The gaps of the unknown close to become the known.* Again, I'm not talking about the kind of space that is "out there." As much as outer space sparks our imagination – the gleaming stars, exoplanets, and other exotic realities that fill our dreams – outer space is evident to us just because it lies above our heads. However, there's no need to distinguish between that immense void and what's between you and this book.

Now, if outer space is the same as our surrounding and inner space, why are we not making equivalent efforts to explore its nature here on earth, right in front of our noses? Could it be that we are lazy to see for ourselves? No one but oneself is responsible for such an endeavor. We can't manufacture instruments to "see" space for us. Is that the reason why we don't want to make efforts towards understanding it?

Let's explore.

We have been taught to conform with concepts like distance, separation, displacement, intervals, difference, and the like – all implying spacing. However, such words only imply coordinates, so they contribute nothing at all to the comprehension of the infiniteness of space. Humans are aware that there is a separation between their eyes, that there is silence between one note of music and the next, that bitter differs from sweet, that there are transitions in temperature fluctuations, and that something is clearly happening between the perfume of a rose and the smell of a rotting creature. Nevertheless, we have mainly taught, and thus conditioned, our kind to see how those words establish the relationship of the observable things. We never inquire whether they have anything to do with the act of observation itself. We have taught our kind for thousands of years that relationships have a quality, but we rarely investigate what determines this quality. Psychologically, it is rather evident when we move from one idea to another that there is space in between. To the mind, the interval between one event and the next – or the image that precedes the following – is what we call time. However, how is time an interval? If space is always between, time is not an interval. An interval would be the space which creates the lapse between one happening and another. *Time is limits, not the space between those limits.* Time is a dimension that operates as a function of space.

Since we have to operate within frameworks, we have a natural need for domain delimitations. In other words, humans need to be able to measure. Now, in regards to space and time, which one dictates measurement? Time is – with its limits – the indicator of measurement. Space seems to be the act of measurement. Is it then, that when the observer observes, such act changes his relationships or expands them?

Spiritually, we all seek something that lies beyond. However, the very word "beyond" implies the presence of a limit. After a limit there can only lie space, otherwise it wouldn't be a limit. Therefore, in our endless quest for spiritual peace, we must inquire whether there is space between us and peace. Meaning, is peace something reachable? Is there us, then a particular space to cross, and then peace? Or is peace stillness, tranquility, and the nothingness of silence? Is space peace? For example, when at war, the generals might say, "Let's call a truce." If they cease to fight, there is a gap in the act of war. In that gap lies peace. When things are rough between one and our spouse, one might say, "I need some space," and in that space one seeks peace. In both metaphors, though one physical and the other psychological, the implication of peace is that it is a spatial property. Throughout history, fundamental shifts have come from peace. No change can ever be achieved without peace. To cease conflict, which is to stop it, is to bring space into the equation. Every change in the entire human consciousness emerges from space.

To visualize this, let's do a rather simple exercise together. Imagine you are required to make some bread. You are provided with a spacious kitchen, an oven, an apron, dough, and all the necessary tools. However, the dough came inside a box, and you are asked to work the dough only inside the box. You are allowed to put your hands in, but you cannot take the dough out until it has the right shape and consistency for the oven. As you accept the challenge, you learn that the dough occupies every single millimeter inside the box, so there's no room for your hands to enter the box in the first place. In such a scenario, you don't just have a constraint, but an impossibility.

The absence of space in and around the dough doesn't allow you to transform it into bread.

Now, let's imagine the same scenario, but you are given a larger box. You are still required to work the dough inside the box before taking it to the oven, but this time the dough occupies about two thirds of the area inside the box. It won't be an easy task; nevertheless, it is possible to do a decent job, so you end up with a piece of imperfectly shaped bread. Finally, let's imagine a third scenario, in which you are given the dough on a pastry board; no box involved. Now, you can prepare the bread however you please and do it anywhere in the kitchen. Consequently, you end up with a nice, warm baguette. This might seem to be stating the obvious. For all of us, it is more than evident that physical change requires space to take place, but the problem arises when we don't concede that psychologically, such an event isn't any different than in reality.

One doesn't need to be taught that occupied space is the impossibility of new outcomes. Probabilities multiply because there is room for them to take place. What I'm trying to get at is that psychologically, in the workings of the mind, it operates just the same. Inwardly, space not only gives rise to new ideas, but by moving facts around, it gives thought a much healthier direction. In some abstract regard, to observe the movement of the mind, and the way of space in it, is to observe the way of movement in the physical world as well.

The word relationship implies closing a gap: bringing together. I just expressed that psychologically, we create our world through a series of relationships and images. Knowledge relies on space, but it takes place when such space is filled instead.

Knowledge is occupied space. If two or more aspects of reality are too far away from each other, they bear no relationship because they're not directly connected. In the same way, if they get so close as to become one, the relationship will be over as well. A balanced relationship is one where both preservation of the essence and change of the framework are possible, and that is a function of the observer. Meaning, to have a peaceful and balanced relationship with the world, one must be able to change.

The most fundamental concern of the human mind since the beginning of our era is, how does one change? *Even the question of death is a matter of change*. We wish for happiness and wellness. We long for a shift in direction, but we don't ever question where it would spring from. There is the change in others and the change in ourselves. There's random change and the imposition of the new, and there is calculated decision-making, which is continuity of the factual. But, all of them are subtle forms of the same activity. Change is the movement of a relationship in the direction of expansion. Inwardly, there is no such thing as gradual movement towards a direction. In thought activity, there is just instant change, which is the immediate end to a relationship. Over the ages, religious and political leaders have promised humanity a different world. Many have come to change us and failed. The nuances of history are many. Men have shaped the course of an entire planet's ecosystem and created rockets that can take us to other worlds, but none of that changes us fundamentally.

When one sees the limitations of our individual conditioning, the natural reaction is to feel compelled to escape that condition, which is to expand one's limits. It looks as if wanting a different way of living is the condition itself, because to want something is to basically put a limit on everything else. It is very hard for most of us to see it, but the procurement of inward change is a clear manifestation of the human condition. Psychologically, there's just choosing. For the human consciousness, there is instant integration of thought, which is creativity, and instant disintegration, which is the death of such thought; that is, there is no graduality, no order, no security, and thus no decay to consciousness. The mind itself will never experience the future because no thought can be sustained so that we see it "getting old." Still, we insist on seeking a wholesome life by mechanical means; consciousness is non-mechanical. So, humans ask, what does it take to change?

First, people have to see for themselves what is limiting their decision making. When we observe, something rather interesting happens. When we see, intelligence takes place simultaneously. The word intelligence means to choose – or read – what is in between. In other words, it is observing what lies above and below, right and left, outside and within, and pretty much all that takes place before and after the observed. Thus, intelligence has its place at the edges of a relationship, beyond limits, where space lies. One could imply that intelligence is not only the seeing of limits, but the activity of changing them too. The human miracle is to see for ourselves what it means to read that which is in between.

Intelligence and peace don't come from order, nor from chaos. Intelligence and peace escape time, so they are outside all margins. There's as much intelligence in order as there is in chaos. Peace is always lying between. The problem arises when one confuses peace from security with the pleasure that comes from control. We usually associate order with control, which breeds a false sense of security, and that is not peace. To experience security is to experience peace, and there cannot be conflict in it. But, *to actually seek security in the affirmation of what will happen next, is the definite root of all human conflict*. We order things so that the outcome is a desired one, and we call this security. This specific activity is time's favorite game.

The basic condition of everything in the universe, including life, is time – because it is the first thing (the beginning). Time acts in the observer by providing the goal of surpassing itself. That is, the observer's activity is to go beyond time. It is not that the observer seeks to know what there is after, but that to observe is to actually surpass time. The universal condition of all living things is to go beyond their own limits, to evolve, and that is an act of escape. Nevertheless, one needs to be careful with the "escape" statement because it might lead to unavoidable paradoxes. For example, if escaping our condition is a fundamental part of our condition in the first place, succeeding in imagining the act of escaping would be itself the first coordinate of destination. But such an image is a moving target. At first glance, it appears as if we are just chasing our own tails, and we all might be. It is all the work of time when it is conceived as a property.

Time is a measurement, and it is a non-moving entity. It must be so because it is a reference, a set of limitations, and as a framework it cannot possibly be on the go. Whatever movement is there, which is always in the present, is impossible to catch. Since motion cannot be measured, it simply can't be the result of time. The present is pure activity, it only observes, and the future has happened only in our heads; therefore, time is always of a second ago. The moment you grasp it, it's already gone, forever a memory. Time lives as a relationship in the function of all things, but it dies instantly in observation.

Along the lines of intelligence, peace, and observation, one is pushed to talk about other aspects of reality that seem to be forever locked in the present as well. It is the matter of beauty and gratefulness. Beauty is one of the most misunderstood human assessments because it traditionally relies merely on images. As previously mentioned, images are all kinds of distortions in the field of observation to which we hopelessly relate. We are taught from a very young age to appreciate ordered images. Symmetry sparks from order, and for most, that is enough proof of beauty. Thus, beauty is associated with "perfect" or complex geometry. Nevertheless, this so-called symmetry from order, which we catalogue as "beauty," will ultimately lead to insecurity in the observer. For some, there might be nothing beautiful about order, as it could represent endless time, torture, and systematic decay. Some others could spot beauty in chaos since it represents the idea of the new coming about, but an orderly fashion is not necessarily new and thus not really beautiful. There are no routes to beauty, and neither order nor chaos are strictly beautiful (or ugly). In any situation, it is evident that what's beautiful for some might not be for others, and vice versa.

Beauty is a quality given by space. The concept of it has been romanticized and taught in poetry and literature for thousands of years. In such a conception, the experiencing of it is just an external factor predetermined by a relationship. And we need to question whether beauty is really dependent on a relationship. Well, if we say so, we have just made it into an image as well. To assign a particular form to beauty would simply not make it dependent on a relationship; it would make it the relationship itself, and beauty is not a relationship. As an image, beauty is just part of memory; it is time and pleasure, and beauty is not pleasure either. So, one asks, what is beauty then? Is it different from intelligence and peace? Let us put it this way: when one is sincerely grateful, isn't it a beautiful experience? Suppose one is not grateful about anything in particular, but one is full of gratitude; is it something that any human being could ever regret? One could regret happiness by the outcome of an event, as pleasurable as it could be, but one could never regret being grateful.

Gratitude is not about any shape, and to be grateful is beautiful. *In gratitude, beauty is at work.* Now, can one be grateful without peace? We saw that peace comes from a psychological gap in time, from stillness. In that stillness, one can be grateful, and this is a source of beauty. Experiencing this is essential to humanity because we receive extensive amounts of energy from it. This is why artists, for centuries, have been trying to capture it, as if they could replicate it. As previously stated, humanity is deeply troubled with making change possible, and that has led us – in the wrong way – to the illusory "harvesting" or "controlling" of aspects which we believe bring about beauty. *What is beautiful can be tamed, but the beauty in it will never be ours that way.* It is thus: there are not peaceful spaces, there is only space. *There are no beautiful objects, but only grateful observation.*

To further expand on the wrongful distinctions we usually make about what space is, or is not, we rely on the fact that space give us dimensions. That is what we have been taught for centuries.

However, to me it is way too evident that the dimensional properties are rather the result of time. Space can't have dimensions because it is shapeless and unmeasurable. Forget about ideas like reductionism. Space doesn't care at all about size. Infinity can't be put on a scale, and space is beyond infinite. You might see the space inside an empty room as measurable, but all you're really seeing are the possible outcomes of events taking place in that space, including placing a ruler with a certain number of units of length. That's what measuring is, just the setting of a series of relationships. Therefore, measuring the area inside the empty room is just another way of saying, "the relationship between the ceiling, the floor, the walls, and the observer as well, is such and such…"

A reflection of the previous can be found in the nature of human language. All that we talk about are coordinates of reference in a plane. These coordinates are related to one another because of time. To illustrate, let's use the word "distance," which implies space, particularly between two or more objects. The origin of the word distance comes directly from the Latin word *distantia,* which means "standing apart," and is composed by two separate words: *di-* *"two, apart,"* and *stare-* "to stand." Since everything that takes place has to do so in a spatial field, one or a series of coordinates is always implied in the meaning of all words. However, words do not define space itself. In the previous example, the word distance simply implies there are at least two things, and they both have different positions in the plane. Say there are one hundred meters in between two objects, the number of meters is the size of "something." "A meter" becomes the unit of relationship between the two objects. Space still remains unchanged and immutable. In other words, distance doesn't determine the amount of space in between, just the function that could take place in it. The amount of space between, or in any direction, is always infinite.

Time sets extremes. It determines point A and point B, the beginning and the end. Properties like "height, width, and length," which are limits, are time, not space. The shape of reality is the shape of time. We have been conditioned to think of time as a rate of change, but change itself is not time either. Change is the reflection of the activity of both: limits (time), and motion (space). Time serves as a reference of movement. Nevertheless, when it "accrues," it acts as a vector, which is an arrow thrown to a specific target. In doing this, time resists the division of space, and that leads to what we see as deterioration. In reality, space moves through time, and that results in the wearing of energy, or the disintegration of relationships. Unlike in the physical world — referring to previous statements — to consciousness, time acts as a limit, but never as a vector. *Time doesn't gain momentum in consciousness.* In the mind, one can see thought moving, which is still space and time interacting, but there is no wastage of energy. This is the reason why "the soul never gets old."

Now, is there anything before space? Is there something in space giving it its function? For example, they teach in modern physics that space bends, and they call that gravity. One can't help but wonder, can a house without walls provide shelter? Or can a knife without a blade cut? Or, in the same way, can a limitless space bend, or have any function at all? Most of us leave these questions alone. We have to pay bills and need to "make a living." The questioning of reality, which is the main human characteristic, is left to the "experts" to explore. We divide the understanding of the world into many disciplines of study, and give authority to those at the top of each division to tell us what reality is about. This current human order breeds more and more division because such authority is granted by an equal (another human), and it makes the rest us of us grow more immature.

The immature mind is childish and correlatedly unreasonable. That is the psychological state of all humans who forsake truth to put it in the hands of the priests or some "spiritual guru." We are never encouraged, from a young age, to delve into what the fabric of reality and truth is. We motivate the young towards the wrong objectives. People are motivated to pursue ideals, and that will lead us to our collective end. Humans' most advanced evolutionary edge is our access to the field of consciousness, yet we spend very little of our lives understanding what it is. Is consciousness really a field? Is it a place? Is it an activity? Why are we not moving in that direction?

Time gave the lion claws, sophisticated teeth, and exceptional strength. Therefore, the lion does what it does, and it is the best at it. We were given total capacity to stop consciously and observe, that is what we humans do. But, why don't we stop, despite knowing we have to? Why is it so hard for some to just observe? Not to just see facts, that's fairly mechanical, but to observe in actuality what is taking place. We have an extraordinary capacity to discern, but what does it do to our existence? Is observation an activity that happens in any plane? As it was expressed, humans observe through or across space. It seems we are bombarded towards a center – the "me" – to feed the field of the mind. In turn, there is feedback in the form of imitation, taking form first as a memory. Then, replication follows, which is the work of time managing preservation. All of these processes can very well be explored by any human being – in depth – regardless of their educational background. To observe is to humans as to swim is to a dolphin. Then, why are we not pushing our youth in a more rational direction? Why limit the mind of new generations teaching science as truth, or religion as truth, or anything as truth? Knowledge is great, but observation is best. If knowledge is limits, to observe is the breaking of those limits.

We expose our descendants to our laws and their consequences, but we don't ever show them where those laws come from. We have foregone moral questions and their relationship to our ways of living for the pursuit of security. We might even be decaying as species because the law, without a rational origin, is distorting the mind of men and their relationships. Humans are losing creativity in the hands of ideological and irrational laws. Why are we not, collectively, having these conversations? Instead we built a massive ecosystem where business and entertainment are humans' first choice for escape, and when that fails, we go about seeking escape through force and violence. We seek occupation of the emptiness rather than observing it.

To occupy is to fill. To occupy the mind is to pour in content that has been repeated many times over; whereas observation integrates existing limits and makes possible the creation of new relationships. Observation is never a replica because it is not related to anything. It has no limitations and takes place outside all definitions, so it is not time bounded either. To peer into tomorrow is called imagination; it is to watch a projection, and that is not observation. To take a glimpse into yesterday is to watch the image of a memory. *Observation precedes all mechanical movement.* Reality is formed by the observer striking limits. This first related limit becomes the primary point of reference, like a metaphor to which the observer clings to navigate in the plane. Just as relationships are not simply psychological inventions, observation is not just an abstraction. A relationship is two limits; observation is the space between.

Observation in the physical world is the same as in consciousness. It exists even where nothing is. We are aware there is "nothing" because we are able to function outside time. The only activity taking place in no time is the present. To be present is to be attending, and to attend is to observe. All concepts we come up with to describe what we think observation is become irrelevant because a concept is a defined and non-moving entity. The moment one creates a composition, one is creating something that can be spotted. Like space, observation cannot be marked. If the "baseline" of the universe could be spotted, it would mean that space surrounds it, and that space would still be the observation before observable things.

It really Is a simple fact; for a beginning to be, it must be preceded by space. *Whatever is, is not space.* Therefore, the universe is space before anything else, and somehow relationships emerge from it. Now, since any start is set as the beginning because of observation, it means that some "observer" creates that beginning. Direction in time is what conditions, and cannot be without space. Similarly, knowledge about it cannot arise prior to the observation of it. Hence, if space and observation precede time in the same way, how is it that they're both different? Did we just invent two different words for the same thing? *Observation and space are both one.*

Since space is imageless, shapeless, and inconceivable to the human mind, one cannot set an altar in its name, nor any science explains it. Space is the bottom line, the designer and creator of consciousness and reality. Let us now explore what we mean by *"space is observation, and truth is its nature."* It was before the beginning and already at the end.

Existence: What a Man Talks About

Every person has their own opinion as to how humans came into existence, depending on their educational background, religion, nationality, and cultural traits in general. There are a great number of ideas and theories as to how everything came to be, and as to when man became man. The physicist reduces it all to particle behavior, and tries to put it into a "theory of everything." For the biologist it's an evolutionary matter. The chemist boils it down to chemical reactions and the spectrum of those reactions. A philosopher reasons about a baseline that is infinite, yet "reachable." The priest says "God created earth and the heavens, and then gave man a special place aside from all other creatures." For the tyrant, a new beginning is dangerous, and the prophet makes it all about faith and divine laws.

Our teachers guide history lessons based on government guidelines, so the story of our origin is homologated across the population; that is the base of our collective identity, which at the grander scale is called society. Our parents put it all together in a pot and feed us with it, hoping we'll be good imitators or will add something new to it. Who could be right? Science says that moment happened around 13.8 billion years ago, and some religions claim it happened around 6 thousand years ago. Those who brought us into this world were advised either by one or the other, and they in turn transmitted to us what they were taught. The question remains, when did it all start, and why are we here?

Nobody knows and will probably never know when such events really took place. However, the one thing that's sure is that the universe split into infinite parts to open the way for us and life in general as we know it today. We are a beginning that is still happening. Existence is one happening. We like the idea of a universe that started when some "clock" started ticking, i.e., when time began. Certainly, time was a beginning, but not the beginning of the whole of what there is to existence. Movement, or space in action as the present, was already there. In the same way, humans were living beings before being man or woman, but because they separated themselves (i.e., psychologically) from the rest, they became man and woman. The decision of us going, "I am," or "I am John," or "I am my mother's son," and so on, must have been born out of a vector in time, which is an idea. Something fundamentally changed the relationship of humans to the rest, and I question, does consciousness have anything to do with this change?

When we refer to consciousness, we are referring to an activity at a dimensional level that escapes decay and deterioration. *Consciousness is the interaction of space and time without aging.* It is always new and remains fresh. It isn't that consciousness doesn't act within the field and boundaries of time, because it does, but *it doesn't know what the future is.* Consciousness can't experience order, so it doesn't aspire for the particular. Since it is forever immediate, it is perpetually secured. Not being a thing of tomorrow, consciousness can't experience insecurity. When thought is aligned with the order coming from consciousness, it isn't seeking to replicate or imitate such order. It is, directly, such order. Therefore, fear, envy, aggression, and conflict do not inhabit consciousness.

When we procure order, so that we secure our future, we are just procuring the continuity of consciousness. Ultimately, consciousness is that which takes place between thought and thinking. Thought is the past, mere memories. In thinking, the fact and the actual take a direction to give us a close view of what could happen next. Thinking lives in the present, but "resides" in the future. In fact, *thinking is the beginning of future*; it is the beginning of the outer. In the flux of events, time gains momentum, and from there all kind of distortions take place. If the senses are the "antenna" reading the outer world, consciousness is the "antenna" from the inner world. *Thinking is where both meet.*

In observing one's own existence, one realizes there are just three main aspects at the base of the experience: Space, Time, and Preservation/Decay. We could translate those respectively to Motion, Conservation, and Integration/Disintegration; or — from the psychological point of view — we could arrange them as Observation, Knowledge, and Order/Disorder. In the most idealistic sense, one could simply go with Present, Past, and Future. Therefore, in our utterances, we are just scrambling meaning out of a reality that is appearing, conserved, or disappearing, and that is as a result of the emerging or submerging of space. Symmetries in thought, language, or reality are not consequences, but the very nature of consciousness. The universe is not really doing anything else.

In saying that "space submerges," I'm implying that the space between the parts "retracts" their relationships to give emergence to a new reality. The representation of the latter is the physical appearance of things. When we say, "space emerges," we imply the dissipation of matter. As space squeezes outwards, it splits everything apart. In the process of space emerging, or filtering into the field of reality, some energy is shed; one could call it disintegration (or decay). It might seem paradoxical; yet, from the same space arises energy, and new limits appear.

In the process of space submerging, as limits pile on driven by physical forces and relationships strengthen, what we call matter takes form. All relationships are born out of the contiguity of limits. When time accrues momentum, space is no longer, and brings what's related together. Decay is consistent, but the resulting scattered energy is not. The work of time is to increase the integration of energy until there is a new function or the strengthening of an existing one. On the contrary, we could say the absolute disintegration of the relationships is the interruption of time as a vector in their function.

Conservation is not integration nor disintegration. In conservation, space and time seem to be in balance. However, in time's efforts to keep the integrity of symmetry, which is a disguised form of replication, deterioration and disorder take place anyway. It just takes a certain number of events to manifest at the "shell" level. To the observer, a relationship ends once it no longer serves its function. Likewise, all human relationships end the moment that the device of interaction (which is the human body) wears to the point that it is no longer able to keep itself together and loses its ability to function. Ultimately, the body, just like a star, fades away, split infinitely by space.

In regards to the human existence, in order to say one "is," one first has to actually know one exists It seems like a dull statement, but in fact it's rather imperative to be conscious of one's own being before any rationalization of one's existence. There are other beings aside from humans that seem aware of their existence, but it is not possible for them to verbally communicate it; thus, the extent of such awareness is unknown to us. *Therefore, language is the closest we have to the measure and scope of consciousness.*

It is necessary to realize what "exist" means in order to grasp what the very purpose of the, "I exist," is. Now, the fact that a person hasn't ever delved into the question of existence doesn't mean they're incapable of distinguishing reality. Anyone must be insane, when asked whether they exist or not, to give a "no" for an answer. By definition, it is more than intuitive to say that one exists. Nevertheless, when a person is asked what it means to exist, most people would likely say something like, "It means I am here," but, what does "here" mean?

In the context of existing, one acknowledges "here" as the time and place where the being unfolds. To exist is an event, and all events need a time and a place where they actually happen. Straight off, one realizes that existing is a coordinate. For man to exist, he must know his place in relation to the rest, or at least to that which is next. He has to know where he stands. The issue with this view is that the great majority of people see the *place* of the happening as the *space* where the existing occurs. It becomes a serious fundamental distortion to the understanding of our nature, since by "a place," we are referring uniquely to time. Any coordinate is a reference, and as previously mentioned, all references are images, all images are limits, and any limit is time. Therefore, in the context of the latter, when we say we exist in a time and place, what we are actually saying is that we exist in *time and time*. It would be even better to say something like, "we live from a beginning to an end." What seems to be irrevocably clear in regards to existence is that man needs at least a first coordinate of reference. Therefore, *to be* is to enter a certain vector of time.

The word "existence" originated from the Latin word "*existere*," which means "to come into being." It is composed by combining the Latin word "*ex*," which means "out," and the word "*sistere*," which means "*to take a stand*." So, to say one exists is to say one is "*taking a stand out*." The natural question which follows is, out of where? If to say that "out" is *here and now*, then what is the "inside?" To the question of existence, it seems all roads lead to a *before and after*, or to an *in and out*, or a *here and there*. Again, human existence is bounded by coordinates. Without coordinates, man would simply be unable to operate, or at least not under a conscious order.

In that spectrum, all living creatures possess some level of awareness or consciousness because no living entity can operate outside the boundaries of certain domains, which are limits and order. However, such a level of consciousness, being less than that of humans, does not carry out the necessary changes that develop the more sophisticated devices we own. For these reasons, there are no dogs making art, trees doing science, nor fungi giving speeches. Nevertheless, all sentient beings have in common their capacity to relate via limits and navigate the field of reality. It means that for any living creature, the activity of space and time must be embedded in the very root of their essence.

Consciousness does not require a mind to create the abstractions we call "shapes" in the universe. However, it does rely on a mind to perform the function of creating life. *A mind is the beginning of all possible vectors*, and for any entity to be considered a living being, it must be able to observe it. Additionally, it must seek the expansion of limits via devices, whether by promoting changes in itself (i.e., evolution), or by developing extensions to its reach (i.e., language, technology, etc).

Take bacteria, which some people would categorize as not conscious, that travel through the field via chemical and temperature fluctuations. The word fluctuation means to undulate or move in waves. A bacterium, which is itself defined and limited, through space interacts with the limit of waves. After striking a wave, it experiences a pause, which allows the observation of the limit of the next wave. Such a repeated process, and the amount of space between waves, determines the level of agitation in the parts of the bacterium. The more space between waves, the slower the vibration. The less space between waves, the more agitation. The whole process tells the bacterium – among others – whether it is too cold or too hot outside, which in turn assists in the decision on what particular path it should take in the field.

In the case of man, time developed a device that is more powerful than any other on planet Earth: the human body. *All living bodies are sets, or collections, of subsets that make up the limit of a particular consciousness.* Bodies are themselves the means by which the mind creates its act of replication. In the case of us humans, a wide array of tools emerged as a result of the path consciousness gave to our development. Time, in its act of preservation, procured image-forming devices (i.e., the brain) to interpret present forms, and evoke past events with the goal of giving us a vision of what has not yet happened. In other words, humans have a great ability to create a vision of the future, and more importantly, the freedom to act on such a vision.

We experience existence concretely, with immediacy. However, since our attempts to catch such immediacy are pointless, we always process it as an abstraction. Over time, our consciousness devised a way to communicate such abstraction. It manifests itself through symbols or images, and out of that set of symbols emerges a flux of information, which is a distorted replica of consciousness we call *language.*

Language is one of those emerging properties of reality that comes directly from our consciousness – not from the mind. Any form of language, whether written, mathematical, artistic, etc., is an abstraction of consciousness, meaning that language is the reproduction of the content of the observer. In some regard, is not that language can manifest skipping the mind, but that it is itself the mind in the outer. Language requires a mind, but the order of it doesn't. If one sees language itself as a device, one realizes that consciousness is attempting to multiply via symbols or images, and via pretty much all human activity dependent on a living-to-living relationship. Language is undeniably conditioned by the building blocks of reality; therefore, man must speak about the building of reality before speaking about anything else.

In space and time, reality gets integrated or disintegrated, consciousness emerges in between. Hence, in trying to create a replica of itself, what consciousness does is what time does. In trying to deconstruct, it does what space does. In trying to preserve itself, it aims to imitate that which lasts through symmetric relationships; and although it doesn't wear itself off, it wears the means out (i.e., the speaker) and then distorts the rest of the field of reality.

To say language emerges from consciousness as if it "evolved" out of it is to oversimplify its real nature. Language evolved out of time. It serves a function to the body, and the body itself serves a function to consciousness. Language is basically an extension of the human body. Through it, consciousness directly accesses other consciousnesses. In language, time could either gain momentum by effectively reaching the other, which brings us together, or it could be defective by the shedding of some of the parts of the abstracted replica of the mind and breed conflict, which is division. I'm simply saying the language man talks is the language the universe talks.

The way the universe constructs and deconstructs is just the way man constructs and deconstructs. At its most essential level, language is nothing but a two-way mirror. At the core level, we speak about time and space because that's both the limits and movement of our content. The property of time and the actualness of space must be built-in in everything we humans talk about. I'm not saying that the context of a conversation is space and time, as if it was certain metaphor; rather that the words themselves in their structure, meaning, and form are space and time.

So, is it all about the void and limits, and that's all there is to it?

The Answer to it All:
Don't Search Between Lines but Between Words

Many experts in the field of linguistics assert that language is the result of cultural traits. They see language as a symbolic representation of how and where one lives. Culturally, we are brought up in customs that reflect the aspects of life that best fit within the framework of values of the society in which we develop. We create symbols in reference to the things which have a common value to us, and communicate them depending on the need. Some other experts affirm that language is an inherited ability; that language is biologically embedded in our DNA. One can't help wonder, what is language really? Not what the studies show about its structure, but rather in one's own experience, what is the word? It is not a question about semiotics, icons, pragmatics, or semantics. We are not talking about syntax, grammar, nor any other structural form or rule that builds up the science of linguistics. Let's not even take what constitutes the particular shape of a message, which is merely knowledge. The question one should pose to oneself is, what is *talking*?

While it is true that culture produces symbols particularly significant for specific groups, the most fundamental flaw one sees in the view of culture giving rise to language is that culture itself is a symbol. Therefore, something must have given rise to the symbol of culture in the first place, and that couldn't possibly have been culture itself. That which created culture, and the membrane of it, must have created language as well. On the other hand, if one sticks with saying that language is merely a biological trait, then one is implying it only serves biological needs. However, art, poetry, music, etc. – which are not biological but psychological abstractions – are also part of language. The shape or the structure of the message becomes obsolete once one goes beyond signs and symbols. Biology, psychology, culture/social sciences, or any other field of study are also old versions of their actual understanding by the time they aim to teach their content because they themselves are abstractions, or symbols. In other words, language created the division or distinction we call science, and now the abstraction – as it didn't have it already in its content – aims to explain where it came from.

It seems spoken or written words are a separation of the body and consciousness. *Language is a split from what reality is, towards a becoming of what is ideal.* For that reason, in understanding human consciousness, we are not going to get anywhere by the studying of linguistic structures. If one gets stuck in structures, one is locked in the past. What we should seek to understand to get the best of our relationships is the speaker, not what is spoken. Of course, through the word, the speaker is known. Knowledge, which is the past as memory, is not just important to human language; without it, there wouldn't be language at all. The issue I'm trying to clarify is whether language is a consequence or a simple reflection of human consciousness, and what does that even mean?

While it is a fundamental function of language to document, it shows that no message is received outside the now-ness. To the listener, all messages are sent in the past, but all of them are received in the present. To the sender it is impossible to structure, order, and rationalize what he will say before watching his own content, which is to observe his past. It is thus:

the sender is in the past, the receiver ives in the present, but they both contemplate – also in present time – how the message unfolds as the future.

Take insight, for example, where the message is understood before the image of it. In the function of memory, the "aha!" moment happens after we find the information we're looking for. In insight, such moments happen even before the image of the idea. Any insight, which is the activity preceding the emergence of a new image, cannot possibly give rise to knowledge if it's not space before. Sim larly, language is space before being any word. Although linguistics as a science helps to understand the structure of time in a message, it is meaningless in the understanding of consciousness because that field is both time and space at once. We can't have one without the other. Language is much more than whatever applied methodology the science of linguistics could ever assess.

It is fairly evident that the normativity, the order and the rationality that language shows are not part of a structure only, but rather the result of a flux of the activity of consciousness. In other words, since consciousness is pure order and rationality itself, all the rules and symmetries we have devised in language are just a hologram of that. The manifestation of consciousness as language is the result of deep levels of attention to the content of the inner layers of the mind, and to how insight gives meaning to that mind.

Let's not misuse the word "hologram" by referring just to the reflection of the content of the speaker. What is meant by "language is the mirror of consciousness" is that whatever is being spoken shows the *activity* of the mind and the order of consciousness. At the symbolic level it shows the content, but at the most fundamental level it mainly reflects movement. Since language is an abstraction of what's possible, it is also the function of a relationship. A function only works through the present; it cannot be preserved as shapes, unless such shapes come with instructions of direction. Any instruction, because it indicates movement towards a vector, is an abstraction – and *all abstractions are functions*.

The word abstraction comes from the Latin word "*abstractionem*." It is composed by the Latin prefix "*ab*," which means "off, away from," and the Latin word "*tractus*," which means "track, drag, pull." Abstraction implies the stopping of the motion of the limits in a relationship, or the changing of such motion into another direction. Therefore, since abstractions are dependent on relationships, they must always be within a framework. In language, we call that framework notation, and it principally represents the scale – or the weight – of the function. The two are not separate. The function doesn't create the framework, nor the scale create the function. It is the act of observation that determines the two of them.

Some of us might think the sentence, "*the sky is blue*," not as an abstraction because it is a fact; the sky really is blue. However, it is still an abstraction because "*the sky is blue*" is not the sky itself being blue. To watch the sky and perceive that in actuality it is blue is one thing, but the letters, "*the sky is blue*" are just symbols. One can say, "*the sky is blue*" are four words and describe which ones they are, but the letters themselves are not the sky, and they are not even blue. Additionally, and most importantly, *"the sky is blue"* is an abstraction because it still contains an instruction of compliance from the listener.

Let's ask ourselves why the speaker would say, *"the sky is blue."* It is a fact, so why would anyone express a fact? The speaker is obviously expecting either the consent or the denying of his reality from the listener, and that is an instruction. The message, whatever it is, always contains the instruction of choosing, even if it is just to respond or not. The responding itself is a function of the listener in relationship to the speaker. In other words, symbols or words which relate to one another open the door to the change in the quality and direction of a relationship via *choosing*, and that is the work of time. Consciousness doesn't choose. It provides the proof of "true" or "false," but the choosing – which is direction – is a matter of thought.

Consciousness is not the house, the car, the wife, the baseball game, etc. Memory, which is necessary for consciousness to operate, is all of those things. Consciousness is assistance to time for the movement of that content towards an ideal. Nevertheless, when the ideal arises, consciousness ceases to assist at the mechanical level of moving memory around, and thought takes over. In order to give form to the interpretable, human consciousness must operate before the conceivable. Therefore, before content and direction, it is movement. Language has to behave exactly the same. It must reflect at its most basic level the activity of movement with the limitation of direction. In other terms, *language is purely how space and time look in a speaker's version of the future, as an abstraction.*

To the sender, the receiver represents a time constraint. The receiver is the limit the speaker's consciousness wants to reach, and ultimately break through. However, the "reaching" is a function, so the listener is shaped (he doesn't stay the same) when he chooses the direction in which his limits are going to expand upon receiving the message. To understand is to choose, and *to choose is to expand the limits towards a vector*. Said another way, what reaching is to the speaker, is what choosing is to the listener. Both are exact equivalents as functions; however, as limits expand, they divert in direction. It seems that consciousness, being the same for all human beings, is so clever that it seeks extension in one another. Thus, because the expansion of consciousness is limited by the mind, and the mind is limited by its content, consciousness seeks to reach other minds to grow and multiply in more than one direction. It appears as if the "thing" is talking to itself. Then, as previously asked, not from the field of formal studies but from our human experience, what is it the word is trying to speak?

If consciousness is the *"original human function,"* where space and time combine, then it is the source of direction of all things. Therefore, images, symbols, words, sentences, paragraphs, and utterances in general are just raw abstractions of time and space. We come back to the question, is it all about the *void and limits?* A letter is a shape of related strokes surrounded by space. In writing, a word is also a shape determined by the relationship of the letters in it, with some space in between them. A sentence is a combined set of words also rationally spaced one from another, and a paragraph is a block of consolidated sentences which enclose part of a discourse, and so on. If the amount of space in between letters and words is not rational, letters lose their relationship with each other, disorder arises, and the message loses its meaning. One can't help but to deduce that *it's not rules that make language what it is*. Norms, which later become rules, are the order of consciousness. In that sense, an order is given through words, words become laws, but such laws' aim is to become the order of the speaker's consciousness in others.

It is imperative to emphasize that language as a structure is man's intention to set norms, but a set of the norms is not entirely what appears to structure utterances, as is suggested in the field of linguistics. Normativity is integration, and of course that's a fundamental part of language. However, silence (for example), which is also part of language, possesses no integrated properties. Silence has no parts; yet, the extent of the spread of silence between words and sentences is what makes the integration (or disintegration) of the rest of the content possible. In this context, the lack of silence is integration. Since silence is an entity in perpetual motion, that's why the interaction between the speaker and listener is always in abstraction. Norms, which are time's construct, become limits for both the builder and abstractor of the message. The resulting activity of consciousness is the grouping or splitting of symbols and ideas – you call it *thinking*.

I proposed earlier that *"consciousness is space and time interacting without deterioration."* Then, is it possible to assess whether language is a construction of only dimensional properties in the plane as they attach or split apart? Could one debunk the primitive view of time as "past, present, and future" through the meaning of language? The perception of time as a mere forward movement is a characteristic of a primitive psychological trait, part of the inherited structure of our brain's past.

If space goes in all directions, which it does, then time must also go in all directions. Every center expands or retracts. Integration is the past, multiplication is the present, and division is the future. The content moving across results in new limits or the dissolution of existing ones, and all of it is happening in a perpetual state. The fragmentation of reality never really occurs because *the present is both the cause and the consequence*, at the same time. What humans call future is a worn off version of the past perpetually acting in the present – hence the conclusion that there is no future in the activity of consciousness. In fact, there are hints as to the absence of a future (linearly) in our utterances. The meaning of *"what is"* begins as a relationship, and the edge of that meaning is a continually abstracted destination. One occurs in the past, the other in the present.

Words represent time, and their meaning always leads to one or several coordinates, which are also time. The significance of a word is in its movement, and it is there that space is found. *Its only function is to be a function*. We know motion is actually found in silence across the entire field of reality. In music, just like in language, silence as the spread of fluctuations, or vibrations, is what makes hearing possible. One sound, at a single vibrational level, does not make music. A melody is a melody because of the space between one musical note and the next. Sounds are the interruption of silence. *A sound is a barrier to the movement of silence.* Motion is found in nothingness, in the actual, not in the factual. In sentences, we can also see the role of space in creating motion between words and ideas.

For example, the word "*I*" indicates a coordinate; however, since it is isolated without any other reference, it moves nowhere. Likewise, the verb "to be" conjugated with "I" in the form of "*am*," is a directional reference, but doesn't bear any movement by itself either. Nevertheless, "*I am*" finds mobility in the space between "I" and "am." *The observer through the space comes into being.* Now, say that instead of a letter we have a black dot, "●." The dot is non-referent and a non-moving entity because it has no visible parts; it has no space in it. It represents no direction and no movement. Therefore, in writing, the dot is the end of a sentence, the end of a statement, or the end of movement towards any additional direction. It is then the case that space is silence, is motion, and the totality of the relationships called letters and words.

The single most important fact about language is that words do not exist until man creates them. Naturally, one asks the question, when and how does it start? What was the first word? If life is a series of relationships integrated as a function, what was the first relationship in the human function? Even more so, how did the first function find action in thought without it containing that first relationship? Meaning, one is empty at birth, and even out of that emptiness the human being finds its function. The body, which is in itself a conscious entity, also functions. What I am questioning are relationships at the external level of the whole of man. That is, after being a human, what do we relate to? And, what do we call it? For the naked man, is there such a thing a psychological "primary object?" Are we modern humans any different from the primitive beings we once were? Throughout the ages we have seen the interaction of space and time, and designed our world in that order.

Humans have been directing their own movie using themselves as the main unit of measurement of everything contained in it.

By "directing our show" I mean literally giving direction, which is the combination of coordinates + motion, and that's the order of human thought. To that end, by the time language arises, it's already too late. *Long before speaking, direction would have already taken off.* We are talking about the countries we founded, economic and political systems, religions, laws, all ideologies and the order of every society in general. Nothing could have been possible without time setting its way towards an objective, and all of that result in the accumulation of orders: the order of humans to other humans, *through the word*. So, if language is a human invention as a result of the direction towards an ideal, the question we need to ask is, what is our first ideal or psychological division from the rest of the world? Is it the "me?" Is it "mother," or "food?" Or is it, "man" or "woman?" The fact is that all of it is the result of our relationship with the world. All relationships are born out of the expansion of previous relationships through a function. Therefore, the relationship of consciousness with its contiguous fields leads to the expansion of itself towards a body. In turn, the body amplifies the reach of consciousness to higher orders.

Our bodies can reach just so far as to grab an apple from a tree, whereas consciousness can devise language, which in turn devises the structure of rockets that take us to the moon and possibly other worlds. In other words, consciousness is aware of our limitations imposed by time, but it's also aware that the nature of time is to be permeable by space; thus, consciousness devises time's perpetuation using the mean of space to expand. Time's structure results in the accruing of limits. That is how the universe devises energy, matter, life, bodies, thoughts, ideas, language, and then all of the other external realities. To answer the question of the identity of our primary object, before anything else, one can't help but to observe limits.

Time as a limitation is our primary object. In fact, time is every single organism's primary object of observation.

At first, it seems as if humanity's main constraint is a logistical one. However, our main concern is that we have limitations. In thought, in language, and in the entire field of reality, we are bounded by frames and membranes. Although no one's first word is "time," everyone's first word is born because of a limit. A human's first limit is that which we use as an anchor in relationship to the rest; it is ourselves. *We are ourselves the first coordinate*. We are time, and as time we seek permanence. This is the reason why most of us don't want to die.

Language is a stunt by time to build limits that could endure the ultimate disintegration into nothingness. Our skin and our thinking are the result of a direction that has been preserved through the building of flesh and words. Not metaphorically, but in the most real sense, we are defined as "something" by the form of our bodies and our ideas. *Those are our limits*. Nevertheless, our intelligence doesn't come from our understanding of time. As shown before, man's intelligence lies in between events, between words and lines. From that silence, time arises. When one stops and stares at such a truth, one finds that the whole flux is undefinable. The moment we attempt to describe it, it inevitably turns into words. Observing, which is space, is intelligence.

Time is our source of inspiration; space is our expiration. The answer to it all is in the measure of man, and *to measure is to change the measurer.*

Chapter 2

THE GREATEST HOAX IN HUMAN HISTORY: "TIME"

WITHOUT MEANING, THERE'S NO END.
THE ENDING OF MEANING IS THE BEGINNING OF TIME;
THE END IS IN THE MEANING.

Studies suggest that sometime around five thousand years ago, man started to trace and document the passing of time. Sundials, or shadow clocks, were the choice of preference for ancient humans to track the passing of the sun over the earth's horizon. Obelisks, which are monumental pieces of ancient engineering to track time, are believed to have existed since the year 2,000 BCE. To devise and actually construct these giants back then must have been, both physically and mentally, an arduous task. There certainly were smaller and lighter versions of shadow clocks before humans eventually set their minds to building the more ambitious monuments we see today in archeological evidence. One wonders, for how long before that have we been tracking time? Even more so, how long before the idea of tracking time could the concept of time itself have been born? Time as a physical constraint is not just an idea that was born from man at some point in history. Time gets as real as all limits get. However, if time is limitation, how can it be movement? A limit is actually the opposite to movement. Hence, where did we get in our heads the idea that we could measure time as movement?

Now, if it is not movement we are measuring, what is it that we are assessing? First of all, all measurement has to fit a framework. Point A and point B are always present in measurement. A beginning and an end are indeed the work of time, but this doesn't mean there is movement. Let's see how a calculation that implies movement behaves. Take speed, which is a simple concept implying both space and time, and let's say we have a vehicle that is moving at 100km per hour. In the current understanding of time across all disciplines, most of us would agree, this vehicle is traveling a space of one hundred kilometers in a time span of one hour. However, what is being discussed here is the idea that since time is any limit, and space is all movement, the thing we are actually measuring is time, and only time. Let's see how it works. In the previous example, we have four points of reference. We have:

Point A, which is the vehicle at kilometer X,

Point B, which is the vehicle at kilometer X + one hundred kilometers,

Point C, which is the sun in position Y,

Point D, which is the sun in the position of Y + sixty minutes.

As we can see in this visualization, to measure movement we are just using references. In it, static images of two objects, the vehicle and the sun, are creating a framework of relationships to which we assign a direction. It is a simple fact: there is no such thing as measurement of space or movement. *Time as something that moves is a wrong perception.*

The word *"measurement"* comes from the Greek root *"metron,"* which means *"limited proportion."* The issue is that motion is not limited unless it is given a framework, and a framework is precisely a frozen proportion in time. Then, the dimensional properties, which are a series of relationships with a certain direction, must be a reflection of time too, not space. It is rather a stubbornness to be aware that space is no-thing, and still insist it constitutes height, length, and width. Whatever nothing is, it cannot possibly have any property because a property is the quality of something. Time, on the other hand, has been assigned a pattern.

We established a version of order in which, to secure continuity, we must move forward. In fact, the definition of the word continuity is to go onward uninterruptedly. What we need to internalize is that to continue is not just one particular version of the whole of perception, but a very clear limit to the direction of such version. To put it in perspective, let's zoom in on the word *continuity*. We associate continuity with motion, but it seems to me that continuity is the opposite of motion. Whatever moves necessarily has to change, but that which changes can't be what it was before. To continue is to multiply, which is to reproduce. To reproduce is a copy, and to copy is the attempt of the same. It is only if something stays the same – fundamentally – that it continues. Thus, to continue is to copy for the attempt to preserve what it already is. In this sense, motion is not continuous – nor interrupted. It simply is something entirely different.

Superficially, I understand that the idea of continuing is that if we keep moving forward, along with all other things, time will have a lesser effect on us. Thus, a sense of preservation is the result. However, a much deeper examination of the meaning of the word reveals what was really implied when it was first conceived. It seems as if *continuity* is really the pursuit of a parallel position to the movement of the relative things for which one wishes preservation, in reference to an end. Therefore, continuity itself is not movement, but the seeking of immutability in relationship to other aspects moving in a certain vector.

If that which seeks to continue achieves such a parallel position, and secures staying along with all other relative things, it will continue to exist as it is. This is mainly why to preserve history we must continue in a certain line, but as in the case of the word continuity, our history is the result of a specific version of time. History is the past, and it only finds its place in human utility by giving rise to a greater purpose. The only function of history is to create continuity. Nevertheless, as I just explained, continuity doesn't really lead us everywhere since it is actually a limit. What one calls continuity now will be called history tomorrow because the pursuit to continue is to lead us towards an end anyway; that's the ultimate goal of continuing, to reach an end, isn't it?

Let's look at the whole of time. A limit is any fixed point in space, but a limit is a limit because there is an observer. An observer sees a limit because he sees it in reference to another limit. Two references are the minimum prerequisite for time to be time. In the realm of human observation, the best of such references is a starting and finishing line. The issue we have, or the distortion, starts when we don't see these limits in reference to other additional limits. Actually, this is where our sense of injustice comes from. Life is asymmetric; life is not justified in the middle of two margins. We don't know when we really start, and we don't know what death actually is. We call these unreferenced points in space "unknowns." A fact is the limit of experience, and there is that fact in reference to many possible other facts that are still unknown to us. We tend to call the latter future. The whole process is simply called time.

The construction of reality wouldn't be possible at all if time didn't move backwards as well. Since space is able to move freely in and out of reality, it allows for time to move in and out too. From psychological introspection, it appears as if time going backwards is what makes all integration possible. Pretty much everything that adopts a form does so because of time's capacity to relate limits. In physics, this action takes many names, from magnetism to gravity, or *force* in general. That is, limits form relationships, and in turn those relationships become additional structures of time.

Of course, when we say time goes backwards, we are not saying it is possible to rewind events as if reality was a movie. *To think of time linearly is just an idea.* Being more specific, "*Past, Present, and Future*" as a linear representation of existence is just an ideological construct to create order in our social structures. Time is the past, but as an act, it exists strictly in the present. The present is the parallel instant when all the probable outcomes of any given function are accomplished. The future is just an abstraction of those two. The immediate contradiction which arises is, if all abstractions are functions, and no function takes place outside the present, then the future only exists in the present. It comes to light; time is but an application to all other human inventions. See, just like Nationalism, Christianity, Hinduism, Capitalism, Communism, Existentialism, Nihilism, among others, *time is merely an ideology*. Thus, if time is the past acting through space in the present, *what is really the future?*

The Future

Before anything else, the future was — and still is — the greatest idea any human has ever had. Not a single ideology has withstood the test of fading away like the concept of the future. The future is a becoming. As a matter of fact, we identify as "man or woman," because we thought about becoming that first. Everyone will be called *XYZ,* before they are actually called *XYZ.* That is, to be called *XYZ* is an order, and to give an order, the one who gives the order must have a vision of it first. At some evolutionary point, humans abstracted meaning, and meaning is always about becoming. *The meaning of man is his future.*

What does *"becoming"* mean? The sun sets, the night falls, and the sun rises back up again. The memory of the sun rising up gives us hope that when the night is over a new opportunity will begin. The becoming implies two notions: the notion of the ending of the current, and the beginning of the new. The future, as the becoming, is not just an invention but a human condition. Nevertheless, the word *future* as the next happening must not have been born out of that condition. Things have consequences, but "consequence" is just a word, not the actual consequence. To see the image of a possible becoming is a normal human psychological act, but not to realize that any image before the eyes of the observer is just an abstraction creates a distortion of what's true.

For all humans, seeing the future will happen with or without the word. What really sets us apart from any other animal is that we think about tomorrow. However, thinking about tomorrow doesn't mean that tomorrow is real. There is the tendency to say, "the future is not real *because it hasn't happened yet*." Nevertheless, such a statement is a reflection of immaturity (as a species.) Ideas are a feature of a sane mind, but ideas are not real. To think of the future is not immaturity, but to think it will certainly happen might be. A vision represents a limitation to the rest of humanity's possibilities because it concentrates time in just one direction. The very first fact, for a mind to grasp the most of reality, is to actually be aware that the future is not going to happen because it simply doesn't exist. The moment time loses momentum in a vector, one is free to look in all other directions.

It may be the case that, at the beginning, humans might have even laughed at the idea of *tomorrow*. When it was invented, they must all have been very much aware it was an invention, and what it meant, functionally speaking. Let's picture an ancient human on a beautiful sunny day thinking about tomorrow, but not knowing what to call it yet. He's not thinking about the sun rising; that would simply be the dawn after night. He was thinking tomorrow as the sun rose after that day's sunrise. What did the sunrise next to the previous sunrise mean to him, and why would he have wanted to invent a word for it? It would seem rational to invent a word for facts, like "hands," or "feet," or "sun," or "three," etc. What could possibly be his agenda for inventing tomorrow?

At the beginning, "tomorrow" was practical in tracking cycles. Many tomorrows bring seasons, and so on. However, as time passed, we got stuck psychologically in its structure and language took over the understanding of tomorrow in a mechanical manner. The issue is that the future is not a mechanical device. As it was said, the future acts in the present, and the present is non-mechanical. The present is space and cannot be trapped, like words are. It looks as if the same condition that brought us the invention of future brought us the invention of language. In essence, both language and future appear to be the same in different formats.

One thing is certain, *the future is the greatest lie ever told.* People aren't growing psychologically because even as adults we keep on selling it to them. The idea of "tomorrow" is man's preferred mean of exploitation. One wonders if it was derived from the idea of controlling other men or out of a practical application in daily life? Evidently, both future and tomorrow are just words; therefore, their concepts must have been born out of humanity's need for a different social order. Let's say we know we have to do something tomorrow, why invent a word for it? There's something to do, you plan ahead, and you do it. But, the moment the task needs to be communicated it becomes a matter of social class. He who sees, leads; and, out of that seeing, he structures orders through the word. Those orders are the order of thought, and the order of thought is the order of possibilities.

There isn't anything wrong with organizing and structuring a strategy for finding food. To plan ahead is ok, but when the plan fails, deception arises. I'm not saying that a failed plan is necessarily a deceptive plan, but an unfulfilled vision inevitably outwears the trust in the direction of the result of such a plan. Therefore, the future, as an idea, is deceptive in nature. There's the other scenario where one plans and the other doesn't comply with the order because he doesn't share the vision. What the healthy minded human understands is that the plan, as a vision, is an event that doesn't exist, and the food is ready only when it is ready. There is nothing extraordinary in sharing a vision, so long as one is aware it is merely a game.

Life is not a game, but the believing part of it is. When believing is about the past, it doesn't breed any major issues other than whether people share a common view on the history or not. However, when the believing is for the sake of some human psychological function, which is the shape of the future, conflict is almost inevitable. What about when what is believed is a vision of danger? Say one person sees the entire group is in danger, and the visionary suggests a course of action. Should one just go ahead with the philosophy that the future is but an idea? Let's see. First of all, what is a vision? A vision is a representation of past events adapted to imaginary situations, that's all. Therefore, if a vision is dependent on the past, or knowledge, how does it relate to the future? Well, it doesn't, until it does. The problem has everything to do with choice. *The future is a choice, and to choose is a game.* To say that to believe is a decision, is to affirm that the future is locked in the present time. No choice exists outside the present. Consequently, this proof also shows that the future doesn't exist outside the present.

Let us try a rather simple example to illustrate this idea. Let's visualize we are in a friend's car, driving on a two-lane freeway through the mountains. Our friend is driving, but she doesn't know the way. Since the destination is very well known to us, we are giving her directions. The landscape is beautiful, and the weather is perfect. However, it is getting late, and the road is dangerous. We ask her to hurry up because it gets very dark at night. We advise her, though, not to exceed a certain speed limit, as the road is filled with curves and cliffs.

In such a situation, our friend must choose between slowing down to avoid falling off a cliff, or face the dangers of the road in darkness. Thought is her device of navigation, and through consciousness she thinks rationally about what the right decision to make is. In order to choose what's to be done, she must weigh one consequence against the other. She must compare and assess which path to take. Now, what is she to compare? One's natural reaction as one reads is that she is comparing two sets of probable outcomes.

She's never been to that road, she's never fallen off a cliff, and she's never crashed before in her life. Thus, everything that our friend thinks about the potential results of her decisions is happening in her head. Through images, she is forming a spectrum of possibilities from which to choose. In the unfolding of events, which is the future in her vision, she realizes whether she made the right choices or not. However, as events take place, they immediately become an issue of the past, not of the future. She never enters in contact with what thought has devised for her other than assisting in deciding. She was able to use it in the present but didn't meet it either at a beginning or at an end.

At the base of human experience, it seems that the invention of the future allows for many marvels, but it also allows for all human conflict. *No human conflict is born outside the spectrum of the future.* All of humanity's problems are predispositions to the next happening. We bear no problem in regard to the past. For example, when the memory of a deceased relative or friend strikes, it is their inexistence that breeds trouble. Meaning, them having passed away is as natural as it should be, but the longing of their presence is the result of illusions of the mind, which are projections into an impossible future. Even revenge, which is thought completely trapped in the past, happens because of a projection into the act of vengeance. Since the past is just an image, it doesn't carry any conflict by itself. It is when combined with the activity of the present that it becomes an ideal to be pursued.

Similarly, the present does not represent any opposite or give rise to friction with anything because it is pure action. In the animal kingdom, one sees that a lion kills, eats, mates, and sleeps, all with immediacy because they don't have a tomorrow. The lion doesn't postpone his next meal, and the chance to reproduce is met with urgency. A lion is capable of complex organizational behavior. They execute complicated and structured plans of attack, which means they have a fair understanding of dimensional properties (of time.) However, we have never seen a lion promoting himself or an acquaintance, as the next thing. No one has ever seen a lion selling dreams to its pack. Of course, we are not lions, but we see it is possible to act according to a complex structure of order, even without the notion of tomorrow.

Many animals work for foreseen events. The squirrel stores seeds for winter, birds build nests for laying their eggs, and a bear eats enough fat to store energy for hibernation. Since their lines are not imaginary, they seek to meet their needs in the present time. What animals do is not planned. For them, survival depends on taking action in the present time. What I think there must be for less rational beings is the experience of limitation. They are surely driven by direction in the field, but for them is worse than for us because they're not as conscious about it. Perhaps, consciousness is yelling at us, "now that you've seen it, change it!"

Without experience there is no future. The present is the experiencer and the future's past. We just saw the catch: the future of the present is always the present itself first. There is a misconception that through the present the past is formed, but the reality is that the past is already what it is, and through the present it is either active or inactive. To think about doing something that will give you good memories is not to shape the past but to think about the future. In a certain vector, which is memory, time continues or dies completely. What we ignore will never meet its future, and once we ignore it, it'll be too late when we realize it has become another memory.

See the immaturity of it. Every year, in December, we have Santa Claus bringing our children gifts. Because the kids have met Santa many other past Decembers, they're sure Santa will come this December, but Santa doesn't exist. We cheat our children for the sake of tradition, until they realize Santa is not real, and life goes on. Similarly, we as adults are sure the month of December will also arrive this year, but like Santa, December is just an invention and doesn't exist either. It is because we have seen so many previous Decembers, just like a child has seen Santa coming every year, that we are also sure December will arrive every year. Some people, such as many politicians or religious leaders, see there's a potential for psychological exploitation that can be applied to all aspects of every human's life. We call such exploitation simply "*lying*."

Let's use another illustration. We'll be using a more realistic approach this time. In designing a building, engineers have to perform many calculations to prepare the structure to withstand the forces of nature. Thankfully, as of today, humans have been engineering and constructing buildings for thousands of years, so the accumulation of experience in that direction is vast. We have seen many earthquakes throughout history, so their framework is very detailed. We know what causes them, and someone even went so far as to create a scale from 0 to 9 to describe their scope of action. We can tell right away that an earthquake is clearly a thing from yesterday. If we had never had any earthquakes before, we wouldn't know about their existence, and engineers wouldn't be able to design buildings that could withstand them. However, when they construct a building, they are preparing it for the earthquakes of the past, not for the ones that have not yet happened.

Let's not get it wrong, it is a marvel of human ingenuity that we can build structures that can stand up to such forces, but our vision is too blurry to see that it is not being designed for a strike from the future. We are constantly preparing for replicas, not anything really new. Time is replication because it seeks to preserve. Matter and thought – all human and nonhuman activity – wears off because the replica is never the same. This very fact is the cause of all of the divisions we see in humanity. Our beloved future is decay reflected in the distortion of the ideal, and language is its machinery.

Now, if we know that it is not that the future doesn't exist yet, but that it doesn't exist at all, why keep on selling it? For security? We sell the future to keep order, and provide security in others. We say things like, "December will come with Santa's gifts," or "My building can withstand any earthquake," or "My rocket is the solution to humanity's survival," etc. We sell illusions. Why? Some romanticize it through the idea of hope, but to hope is to also be stuck in some ideal. Hope is so much easier to exploit than the raw idea of future because *in hope there is no choice*. This is the reason why organized religions are so dangerous, and the reasonable man is silenced by the tyrant. But to think there is no hope is also deceiving because a future with no hope is still an image. Even a tomorrow with no purpose is still a projection. Again, thinking is the beginning of future.

Let's not confuse things though; to think is not a delusion, but as it was noted before, to think that what one is thinking will happen is. Memories are facts, thought is illusion, and the projection of that thought in the hope that it will take place in reality is to a certain degree a delusion. *All non-factual forms are abstractions of the next happening*. Someone, in ancient times, conceived of this idea and made it the deadliest weapon ever created. However, as time passed, everyone (all of us really) got caught in their own trap. It appears as if the future was born out of fear, or as if some detriment aspect in the human life pushed us to procure the continuity of such abstraction in physical reality. The abstraction came first in the form of an image in the shape of what's possible, then the word followed.

I raise the question again, could language have made us deviate from the future's true meaning? If we knew from the beginning that the future was always abstract in the present – imaginary – why do we not see it as an idea nowadays? For most of us, it is given as granted that the future will happen, but we know in actuality that it won't. The past gives us dimensions, position, and relationships. *The present gives us function in those dimensions.* What does the future give us? Anything we can come up with as an answer to that last question is going to be (one way or another) just an abstraction.

Just as the future gave rise to language, it has given rise to many ideologies. Under the ideal tomorrow, many ideologies have been created. A robust fact is that all ideologies work the same way as the idea of tomorrow. As much as we want to distinguish and catalogue our ideologies under the scope of different disciplines, they're all subtly modified versions of *"the future."* Tomorrow, the becoming, the change, truth, or whatever we decide to call it, are just psychological limits we invented. Like the lines we call past, present, and future, we draw many lines that don't exist.

Nationalism, sciences, religion, etc., are all forms of the imagination. There isn't anything wrong with science, but it is still an ideal. There is nothing wrong with scientists finding the cure for Polio – thank science for it – but no rocket or telescope has the power to bring peace to humanity. The scientist pursues a better future, a new becoming, and an ideal world where proofs of time and knowledge are at the base of society. That's their own version of truth, but such a version doesn't exist because life is a moving target. The universe doesn't have laws, men do. Scientists use methodology and mathematics to create the laws of the universe, just as the priests use faith and hope to create the laws of God.

The visible pattern is that the future has mutated into language, countries, laws, religions, sciences, socio-economic systems, and above anything, systematic control and violence. If there is anything that can really be called future, as that which is a consequence of the present, it is deterioration and division. The last of the events in reality is division. It is precisely disintegration, physically or psychologically, what we see as the end of all systems. Systems also mutate into other systems. However, let's take into account that a new beginning is ultimately a beginning by itself, and an end is ultimately only an end. That which ends is no longer, and that which begins is unaware of it.

The future as a lie is true – in the word – because its meaning is that it doesn't exist. Therefore, for the conspiracy entertainer, it would seem attractive to say, "*Yes! the future is a lie*", and then exploit his explanation of why it is a lie for his own purposes. That is a great deal of human activity. Look at it this way: that which is false in an instruction brings movement to a halt, but it also ignites another direction, which is the real meaning to the observer. I noted a few lines above that a man's future is his meaning. We want to make something out of our existence because otherwise it feels as if the void could asphyxiate us instantly. We either feel like running away from it and seeking refuge in the comforts of time, or choosing to fight it as means of imposing a secured order, which is anyway a form of escape.

The void is not secure because it clings to nothing; yet, everything comes from that void. I am not suggesting to buy into a purposeless life. I said, that's also a trap. What's being asked instead is, why do we buy into purpose? Meaning itself is not our condition; the seeking of it is. Yet, the moment one gets to one's purpose, one has already become it, and it has no meaning anymore. Thus, it looks as if to perpetually chase our meaning is our purpose. I am inquiring into, why? Then, I see the condition right away in that very "why?" As a species, to understand life's condition is the first step towards maturity. At the bottom, all living creatures live bounded by time, and in humans that condition addressed the creation of our "tomorrow." The moment we understand that, our true capacity to change begins.

If the future is really something, *is the division of time by means of its progression into weaker structures, or relationships, that end up disintegrating into nothingness. Nevertheless, remember that nothingness or space is a center, and such center is already before time.*

... the whole thing is still an idea.

The Known and The Unknown

Knowledge is a field of the past. It comes from one of two sources: imitation or insight. The array of ways to register information is practically infinite, but the registering process is always an act of imitation of the fact. Knowledge relies on memory, but memory doesn't rely on knowledge. To be experienced is to be good at imitating memory. Insight is different. In insight, the image emerges from an internal space, bringing the new to light. Nevertheless, insight becomes a memory too quickly, so even a creative mind falls into the condition of copying the act into a memory. To learn is to inquire, and that brings about insight.

When insight becomes real (i.e., when it becomes physically available for the rest of humans) its outcome brings us great energy. That energy doesn't come from the idea or the object, but from each of the observers themselves, and what it means for them. It was noted that meaning is future, but once the new becomes factual, it enters the domain of time. As the words or objects become a memory, they start shedding its energy off by the act of time. Hence, *to learn is energy, and knowledge is the accumulation of that energy*.

All observers seek the expansion of knowledge in a particular path to avoid the complete disintegration of the facts that conform the already existing structure of knowledge. However, a fact can only lose energy over time. This is why nothing stays the same in the universe. Knowledge is a distortion in the field; it can only grow disproportionally with respect to everything else. Since knowledge is in a direction, it creates all kinds of imbalances. Whatever is already going in one direction cannot go in every direction at the same time. Therefore, in order to grow, and keep itself alive, knowledge seeks to build layers. It grows layers of facts, which will protect it against the perpetuality of motion in existence, which is why we see particular knowledge becoming specialized in certain areas of study and disciplines over time.

The word knowledge can be traced to the Proto-Indo-European root *"Gno-,"* which translates as *"to know."* To know is to acquire; it is the comprehension of a collection of facts. The word comprehend comes from the Latin word *"comprehendere,"* which means *"to take together."* It is formed by the Latin prefix *"com-,"* which means *"with, together,"* and the Latin word *"prehendere,"* which means *"to seize."* Knowledge is a collection of facts brought together. The question would be, who do we seize the facts from? Or, from where do we bring them together? There is insight, which is where knowledge comes from. Additionally, we're seeing that there is something that knowledge seeks protection from. Therefore, there is clearly an aspect of existence before knowledge. Could such an aspect be what gives rise to knowledge in the first place?

The senses are always seeking. The senses are antennas to the outer world that seek to catch information. Part of the mind's job is to store that information. However, the whole of reality is not directly observable, so we have to discover it by abstracting the rest of the facts. Without a quest there's no knowledge. To embark on a quest is to question, and to question is to ask; but again, *ask who*? Intuitively, one is tempted to quickly respond, "ask ourselves." However, if we are the ones responsible for the answers, then why ask any questions in the first place? The issue is that all centers, relative to the observer, eventually leave the field of perception because the space there is absolute and the measure of motion is infinite – or at least that's my perception as a human. *All centers are empty relative to the observer.* Each of us is, at our core, just empty. *Nothing precedes the self.* Pure space, which is pure motion or pure function, is at the center of every observable point in the universe. I'll cover this particular aspect of reality in human perception later on.

Insight is first, then knowledge. Insight means *"to see inside."* Knowledge, which comes from outside, is just a relationship within the activity of insight. All new knowledge comes from within. We all, without exception, have the capacity to inquire, and acquire new knowledge. The center observes in emptiness, and *it is* before all there is to conceptualize. To observe is the twin brother of not knowing, and I think we erroneously invented those two concepts for the exact same thing. It is observation that brings about insight, and in turn insight reduces it all to one of two answers: "true or false," or "good or bad." These two options are the bottom line of all inquiries.

Inquiring is the assessing of going one way or another, and that is a function of whether the direction is the right or wrong one. In turn, those answers expand the entire content of the observer to become part of the self. What is implied by it is that direction might be "right or left" because there is an observer, so all decisions' purposes are ultimately reduced to fit the dimensions relative to the position of the observer. Insight creating knowledge truly feels more of a geometrical issue than a matter of progression.

The shape of a concept is defined by its limits. No concept arises without inquiry. Ideas are the result of the direction internal quests take, and observation is the first step towards such quests. A question is the first limit in the search for answers. The boundaries of what we know separate us from what we don't. Therefore, we need to reach that boundary and "stare" into the unknown in order to generate the emergence of new realities. When one says a question is the limit that separates what reality is and what it is not, it shouldn't be taken metaphorically. Let's see how that quest starts. Let us use question words to see what I mean.

What? is a boundary defining the form;
Where? is a limit in reference to other limits;
Why? is a cause, the limit between what's known and the limit which is still not known;
How? is a framework, the limit that has a relationship with a contiguous one before and after;
How much? is a quality inside the framework;
How many? is also a quality inside the framework;
Which? is an indication for the separation of limits, to exclude the rest;
When? is a limit in relationship to an event;
Who? delimits responsibility.

All of these words have different meanings in respect to their qualities, but they all point to the same thing: direction. All questions are orders to consciousness for answers. If we question other humans, we are ordering them to give an answer. If we question ourselves, we are requesting an answer from our own consciousness. Hence, answers usually come in the form of ordered structures. The more ordered the observation is, the more rational the answer will be. I'm not saying that the quality of order resides in observation. I'm implying that *to observe orders*. For knowledge, it does so in two senses: in the sense of giving direction (the question,) and in the sense of rationalizing that direction (the answer.)

Answers always come from the center, but the center doesn't have proportions. Therefore, it is not clear how it propels insight forward. A middle is measurement, which is time, but a middle is not a center. A center is infinite and rational on its own. It doesn't care about size either because it is already relative to the whole. My center can't be different from yours, neither from the center of an observer at the edge of the universe. Whatever observation is, it must reside in there. How is observation such emptiness?

Let's see, when one sees a flower, the flower is not empty; however, to observe the flower without knowing what it is, is psychological emptiness first. That is, the thing's name is not "flower" at first sight; we instead gave it that name out of nothing. It is thus that any quest leads to a center from which all limits emerge.

We are limited because we are born out of boundaries;
A woman is a boundary; both physical and psychological;
A man is a boundary; both physical and psychological;
Boundaries are limits;
Limitation is the work of time;
Time gives rise to matter;
All matter is a question;
An answer is the outcome of consciousness;
Consciousness is the outcome of observation;

Observation is the work of the void;
The void is the unknown;
Death is the unknown.

The unknown sets out on a quest for meaning through knowledge. I noted before that "the thing" that created the future must be the same thing that created the word "future." Therefore, the observer observes himself, and out of that, time emerges. The center creates the whole of existence. There's even a theory for it in science; it is called "The Big Bang."

One could figuratively picture how the quest works by imagining knowledge as a giant web of interconnected facts. Let's do a thought experiment with it. Imagine each node where the web interconnects facts as a sphere. Each sphere contains knowledge. The web and the spheres are floating flat in the nothingness. Each ball is transparent, so one can see the information it contains. Let's now see ourselves as a little person who can hop onto each ball to look for information. Where knowledge is more concentrated, there's not even the need to jump, and one can simply walk on facts. However, where knowledge starts dissipating, the spheres start spreading apart. As knowledge is more and more diffused, the distance between each ball widens. One, as a little person, starts jumping further and further until the next fact is so far away that one could barely make it. Finally, one is at the furthest point from the known. The rest of the spheres are left back, and one is facing an infinite void. It looks as if by staring at such emptiness, a new fact would spring out of it, and surprisingly it does. A new sphere or fact emerges and we jump on it, adding it to the web of knowledge.

At the beginning we didn't have much. Yet, we built an entire human civilization out of knowledge we created using ourselves as the stepping stone for order. A psychological order translated into a physical order. Nowadays, we have satellites in the outer regions of the solar system, robots on Mars, cures for invisible diseases, etc. We can trace it all back to us. Man invented his world. Then he named every fact, and called the collection of everything "knowledge." The way it all works is by means of references, and references are metaphors. Thus, man creates metaphors so that new facts are born. Later, out of the emerging facts, he would make newer metaphors so that in turn he could bring other newer facts into existence. The process repeats over and over. Without metaphors there is no knowledge. No object in this universe exists without a reference. Time itself doesn't exist without an end.

We base the creation of knowledge on what truth is, and we see truth is tracked down to the center of the observer. We observe, and give names to our observations. Our observations later find function, principally as applications to metaphors that we created previously, after combining them with current facts. One can't help but stumble into silly statements such as, "so, man invents man, then studies man, to later define man." As foolish as it may sound, this is really one of the most common doings in the field of knowledge.

Knowledge is a consequence of learning, but knowledge is much less important than learning. Learning, which is to stop, to see, and to observe, can give us as much knowledge as we wish for. Knowledge, instead, will seal itself into the structure of pride and cause many sorts of perversions in human relationships. Of course, knowledge is great when the application is noble. The greatest and noblest of the applications of knowledge is to keep us learning more, for the learning mind is a mind that is whole, and it aims for freshness and plenitude.

A person who thinks security is found through knowledge becomes stiff and closed to change. The one who is an authority in the field is the pride and pinnacle of the ideal. He, who represents the path, becomes stubborn and bitter. A life full of knowledge is nothing in comparison to a life of continuous learning. In a particular sense, because of humanity's current appreciation of time, we fool ourself into the structure of knowledge. Knowledge can't possibly deliver us security because security is affirmation. Knowledge is the result of affirmation, but it is not affirmation itself. In other words, the abstraction in the order – the present if one wills – is security. That which we are sure of becomes knowledge, not the other way around.

Knowledge brings us closer to truth, only if we're open to change. See, the problem is that special zing too much keeps us away from the truth. When we're caught in our own psychological composition, we either live in the past, or in the flow of some dream. Say we could achieve knowledge about everything – "the universe in a nutshell." Should we ever achieve such ridiculousness, time would stop, wouldn't it? What would be left? To know is to seize time. Every piece of information is a fixed point in the universe. To know everything would mean to fix everything – *all functions would be over.* To not know set the universe in motion. *Whatever not knowing is, it must be the same as movement.*

The Layers of Reality

Reality is, with or without an observer, *is it not*? Reality as a concept cannot be without an observer. For us, reality is in the framework of knowledge. Whatever is describable and/or measurable between two or more observers is real. It's not that for one particular observer reality doesn't exist, but that reality – as a concept – is irrelevant to the individual human life experience. Our conception of reality is strictly intertwined with our idea of time. Everything that time touches is real. However, under the scope of the idea of time as past, present, and future, it is harder to understand reality because we are basing part of our picture of what it is on an event that doesn't exist. This very distortion of reality might be what has produced, and is still producing, so much turmoil between humans.

Our capacity to understand human reality, in a rational way, could be lost because of how we are conditioning ourselves. It is clear that the future is a projection of images, and such imaginative outcomes are not real until they are. Therefore, reality is the past, not the present or the future. In a sense, imagination can only be real as it becomes a memory, and that's possibly the reason why consciousness seeks the expansion of that imaginative reality through our symbols and behavior. The present is not real because it is pure motion; it is the function of the entire reality – or the functioning of the past. The present is neither real nor unreal; *it is something entirely different*. Regardless of how we perceive time, we observe that it is impossible to assess reality without inquiring about it.

The word reality comes from the Latin word *"realitas,"* which means "a *relative thing"* or "*a thing with the quality of relating."* It is composed by the Latin word *"res,"* which means *"thing,"* and the Latin suffix *"-alis,"* which means *"relative to."* Reality is not just time, as we see it has a quality, and qualities are given by space. Nevertheless, we are entertaining a contradiction here, since space is a function, and an abstraction is only possible in action, which is present time. One might ask, what is the problem with reality being a thing in the present? The issue is that, as pure action, the present can't be a "thing." Thus, measurement of reality in actuality is impossible, and *without the possibility of measurement, there is nothing.*

The solution to such a problem of perception is to simply take the present out of the picture of time. Let's say the present is the moving of the past. Out of that movement an abstraction emerges. We know abstractions are attempts to replicate something. Out of that attempt to multiply, the fact loses energy in proportion to what it was previously. In the long run, what's next is always deteriorated in relation to what it was. One after the other, each fact is an older version of the one that preceded it. Why would the universe seek movement of the past? Well, no one knows, but at least we can assert that without movement there are no qualities.

What is the role of quality in reality?

Quality gives us colors, temperature, sounds, smells, and flavors. Movement gives us emotions and sensations in general. Quality is dependent on the speed of motion, and as the rate of velocity varies, forces start to manifest (or dissipate) in different arrays and forms. Both speed and velocity are determined by time. The more momentum time accrues, the longer it lasts in a specific direction. Put another way, psychologically, the more knowledge about a subject that is accumulated, the more of a truth the subject becomes; thus, the longer it lasts as a fact over time. What's more, physically, the more time builds up in structures, the more orderly they are, and the more secured over the ages they become.

Contrary to current understanding, I suggest to anyone interested in a different framework of reality, to explore a version of time which either 'obstructs' movement, or 'allows' it, meaning that it is not merely motion. The more permeable it is to space between its parts, the faster the structure "dies out," but the more it limits movement, the longer it lasts. Thus, *the whole of time is the whole of its layers.* The more symmetry there is in the structure of each layer in relationship to the previous one, the greater the chance of preservation. *Space in reality is an irrational constant; yet, it is the source of rationality because it fractions equally everything apart.* It doesn't really go faster or slower, but instead more or less of it is constantly going through the geometry of time.

What determines the accumulation of time in a vector is the strength of its relationships. It is clear that the quality of relationships is their speed and velocity, but what determines the relationship in the first place? The word relationship comes from the Latin *"relationem,"* and it means *"to bring back."* Relationships are dependent on the length of space in between them. However, we know that space doesn't actually have length, so what is more – or less – space? Let's recall from previous assessments my suggestion that space is observation, and observation relies on the reaching or meeting of a limit. The reaching is a function, and it is supported by how close or far away the observable limits are in relationship to the observer. Psychologically, length of space is most likely to manifest as what we call "*a need*," or "*desire*." Physically, for any given observer, that length is pure probability of possibilities. In both cases, space is a structurer, and time is the structure.

I can't say what space exactly is, but I'm certain that it must be the same as to not know; and, that very not knowing is the observer generating motion through the act of observation. The resulting activity is a consciousness that seems to always strive for symmetry. The more symmetrical, the stronger and more stable the features of reality; thus, the more permanent they are. *Observation is some sort of "artisan" of reality.*

Why is it that nature seems to favor symmetry?

Symmetry is balance. The order of consciousness is balanced and rational. Rationality means to ration: to cut proportionally or into identical parts. We tend to like people with symmetrical facial structures, we get hypnotized by the shape of diamonds, and the sphere – which is the most symmetrical structure known to humans – is also outer space's universal form of preference. From far away enough, objects will always seem round. All beginnings must start with a 'spherical' relationship. Take the number zero as an example, which is represented by an oval. Zero is at the core of all numerical notion, and it represent nothing. Zero is the peak of symmetry; yet, it can collapse any mathematical function at will. It lacks a beginning, but it finds its end in number one. *Zero, just like any center, is not really number but a function.*

Symmetry is nature's chosen tool to fight the disintegration of structures. Take stars as an example. Stars have the quality of lasting for long periods of time because they are massive objects with strong structures. Time has done its job on them, but even stars fade away into nothingness. With time lying on top, layer by layer, the atomic composition of a star decays. Every movement of the life of the star is a new version of it, displaced into a new possibility. The battle between space and time seems to always have the same winner. Eventually, because of the loss of energy, the star loses integrity and can no longer maintain its composition.

Metaphorically, it seems a fair resemblance to compare an exploding star with a balloon being filled with air from within. A star dies, leaving space, or rather extremely symmetrical structures in its place. Another visual representation is that of black holes, which are structures so complex that not even light escapes their reach. Current knowledge tells us that gravity is what causes such an effect on light. Nevertheless, even if it ends up being mere speculation, here it is being proposed to further examine whether symmetry is the result of time's success in the accumulation of the limits which give them their mass – which in turn creates the effect of gravity. In other words, symmetry seems to be the main contributor to the preservation of the limits which form reality (including physical mass.) It could be said – non-scientifically – that in black holes time has created such a vector that these objects become "impermeable." Meaning, space has much less way through them relative to the observer. Since probable outcomes rely on space, the more symmetric and the more layers of time they possess, the more their probability of changing reduces. Therefore, time accrues much more "slowly" around the field of disturbance of these objects. It looks at first sight as if, for time to resist change, the justification in the composition of the building blocks of reality is the most important of all factors.

The previous examples were not to show specific aspects from the perspective of any particular field of science, but instead are meant to serve as metaphors for illustrating a different angle to our current version of time. I think we need to explore the possibility of a version of reality where psychological relationships prevail over physical ones because one is the result of the other. Meaning, a version in which geometry is much more important than time. Keep in mind that geometry is not necessarily time if time is given only a forward linear property. In that regard, there's geometry in the past, present, and future; however, there's not past, present, or future in geometry. That is, it is strictly necessary to have geometry in progression, but geometry can definitely be without progression. The past is geometry, and it seals or limits the perpetual motion of the present. On the other hand, if we concede that time moves freely, then geometry is time and vice versa.

We can make use of a more subtle or more mundane example of the above: our relationship with a glass of water. Say one is thirsty, and one is presented with a glass of water. One doesn't even have to make a choice as to how or when to pick the glass up. One simply reaches it with one's own hand and drinks. Now, let's say one is in a room, and the glass is in another room. The distance was increased, and automatically the relationship changed. Although one now has to make a decision about whether to stand up and walk to the other room to pick up the glass of water, no trouble really arises because the movement effort to that end is still minimal. Imagine a third scenario: one is in the same room, but there is no water at all in the house. One has to dress up, comb one's hair, drive to the supermarket, park the car, buy the water, drive back, etc. In this scenario, not only the distance between one and the water changed, but also a new series of decisions are to be made, like how to dress, which road to take to the store, where to park, etc. Finally, say there is a fourth scenario, in which one doesn't have a car to drive to the store. We see where this is going. Space changes the quality of our relationships, and any relationship is always time. Even in this simplistic view, one can't help noticing the change in that which is related was not just psychological, but also physical.

Humans place a higher value on things that last longer than those which last for a short time. Understand that the goal is not entirely the continuity of the desired object, but the preservation of our own psychological security. So long as we feel secure, we value more the durability of the thing that's creating such security. In other words, is not the lengthiness of the object/objective what we seek, but the status quo of our sense of security. Quality is highly valuable to us. The more quality, the stronger the relationship. There is only one way to achieve the right quality: through observation. As a psychological factor, the more potential a desired outcome has to become real, the more wished for it is. The faster relationships are built, the more time there is for us to buy into reality, and the more layers time can lay in such a direction. The same is true in the opposite order.

If time is humans' primary condition, why don't we have a specific device for detecting it? We have many types of clocks of course. We have sundials, mechanical and electrical clocks, and we even have extraordinarily precise atomic clocks. However, a clock doesn't detect time as we detect sound or taste. A clock is a metaphor we use to enclose some change in relationship to the frame of change of other objects. A clock doesn't give us a sense of life. Instead, life itself gives us a sense of time.

Time as an idea is not different from the idea of death; hence, the human error is in seeing time as the cause of death. Both aspects of reality are interlinked, but death is not gradual, as time is. Death is part of reality, but it just is or is not. Therefore, what could the biological device that gave us the conception of time as we know it be? Animals get old just like us. They see themselves getting old and closer to death, but they don't generate abstractions of a possible hereafter. Where from, then, did we get this idea of progression?

We know all ideals lie at the end of desire, or at the ending extreme in a line in time, which is always a future limit. We are aware that the ideal doesn't really exist, so why then do we pursue it? Our condition tells us, *"Go this or that way,"* and at the same time the condition also says, *"I am just a condition, just a desire."* Metaphorically speaking, the time part of ourselves has to able to 'see' itself in order to recognize that in that very perception lies the next relationship in its content. The most striking fact about our reality is not how it all works, or that we understand how it works; it is that one observes oneself seeing it working. The observer seeing tself in the field is the beginning of time, and he who observes is the measure of it.

Every observable point in space must be unrestrained by direction before it becomes time. However, in the order of humans, we are not capable of grasping a physical existence where existence moves freely in and out of reality. Like multiple ripples in the water, merging into each other, consciousness is not linear. Consciousness' activity just is, or is not. Our fixation with it is that only one observer at a time can access it. Only each of us ourselves has access to the place where order is sparked. In reality, our obsession has more to do with control and dominance than with consciousness itself. Not even in our wildest dreams could we see what it would mean to ever be able to put our hands on the thing that orders the entire universe. Fortunately, in a mechanical way, we will never be able to do so – at least not in a way that our current biological and psychological condition permits.

The way we create reality works by layers. The inner part of an outer layer is always an outer layer of a yet-deeper inner one. Still, our relationship is always with the outer, until we turn observation towards the inner. The inner layer is considered inner because we relate it to an outer limit. For example, take the human body, with its legs, arms, hands and head, and all the rest of it. The skin is the outer layer, but if we turn attention to the inner parts, we see organs. At that point, the skin of the body becomes just a reference, yet the shape of an organ is not the whole of the organ. The whole of it is its shape and its parts. Hence, we now turn our attention to the inner parts of the organ. Below its layers there's blood, and inside the blood there is the cell, and so on. We have tried to "peel" or map reality, through many methods of study, in order to see if there is such a thing as a layer of consciousness.

We have tried everything – from neuroscience to quantum mechanics to mysticism, and others besides – but everything seems to fail. Reducing reality, layer by layer, doesn't seem to be helping. There's always a point where reality leaps, and we can't quite make the connection that creates a continuity from the inner psychological order of events to the order of stuff outside our bodies. We see the continuity in the entire process. One sees that there is an order, and then the coherence of the given order in action, but that's it. That's precisely the reason why we live in abstraction, or locked in the present. It could be that our documented studies of the outer are just a reflection of the behavior of the metaphors we create, but that doesn't seem to be the true nature of reality.

Let's do a fictitious illustration. One has been given a pair of eyes, which is our body's instrument to detect light, but let's imagine that one has been given an extra sense that allows the perception of "stuff" smaller than a photon. We now know there is space between that new sense and the sense of sight, and such space is the function of the new sensation we are perceiving. Time in that function has to go about much faster in order to precede light. We observe that n order to detect taste on our tongue, we need some number of molecules of the food. Most importantly, in tasting, we need the food to remain in our mouths for a fair amount of time in order to make sense of what we are eating. Similarly, detecting smell takes time; however, since molecules float in the air, we are almost constantly being bombarded with odors. In hearing, sound waves, which move much faster than food and odors, keep us hearing almost without pause. In the case of light, the fastest and smallest perceivable object to humans, our relationship is instantaneous. Light, unlike sound waves, can travel through the vacuum of space across the entire universe. However, even light decays because it has composition. In other words, there's space in between its parts.

In the previous, what's meant is that the smaller the layer of reality we detect, the quicker the relationship is established, but the quicker it also fades. The movement of the smaller moves the larger, but the one of the larger necessarily drags the smaller. Consciousness moves us, and we carry it over with us everywhere it sends us.

Although we don't feel consciousness in the conventional sense, we know it's there because it shows us the shapes of the light. If we say consciousness is a field, a real thing, then it can be detected. Consciousness could very well be a sense in development. In a dog, time made its job of addressing smell as a vector of observation more of a focus than it did in us. Hence, we don't smell as keenly as a dog, but a dog doesn't think as rationally as a human. Likewise, it could be the case that the more we pay attention to consciousness, the more we will develop the biological tools of access to different domains of perception.

The view of us controlling consciousness is a misleading one. If it's ever accomplished, then our relationship with it will change. If we change our relationship to the field of consciousness then a higher order becomes established – another layer – as a consequence of the expansion of our observational domain. Whatever consciousness exactly is, it is the smallest and fastest field of interaction relative to any given observer. Meaning, for consciousness to become of our physical dominion, what is giving it function would need to become our new base field.

Such a new field would then be our primary order; a new set of laws. What secrets such a field could contain sparks the imagination. Such a type of cognition could potentially give us much better access to the quantum world than the one provided by any electron microscope or particle accelerator.

If perception is relative to position and motion, we need to ask in regards to the question of plenitude and wholeness, what place do we have in the universe as a whole? And, what does such questioning do to our meaning? I'm asking, is meaning the same across the entirety of existence? Not the result of meaning, which is a reference, but what meaning is itself? Outwardly, what place in perception does the edge of time have with us and with meaning? Aren't they the same? It seems so, but scale complicates things. Scale is a problematic factor in perception, but it's not an issue for meaning. The farther away objects are, the more static they seem. Our relationship with stars is not as dynamic as it is with other people. Reality is built with time at the base and on top, and space as 'nothing' before and after all limits. Limits strengthen or break. There is movement, fast or slow, and there are stretches of space depending on the position of the observer. The universe, just like anything else, is a framework. Physics excels at explaining all of this, but it fails miserably when it comes to matters regarding the act of the observer and the present time.

No matter what we wish to make out of all of the things we could ever know, small or big, fast or slow, beautiful or ugly, beginning or end, there's only one truth in reality. There is only one truth for all observers, and that is space. Not knowing has its magic; or, there's some magic in not knowing – literally. Space could be called the *"null constant"* of reality. However, because in the end *nothing stays the same* and *nothing lasts forever*, this feature of reality is what gives us whatever beyond infinity really is.

In our daily lives, reality addressed to a specific end achieves many names within the spectrum of knowledge. Depending on qualities, humans categorize reality. We label it, organize it into subcategories, and we find applications for those findings. Physics, Astronomy, Chemistry, Mathematics, Medicine, Economics, Psychology, Philosophy and Linguistics, among many others, are some of the labels we assign to the ideals born out of understanding. All of it is the job of time, but deep down and most fundamentally, it is the work of observation. *The thing that is organized, the organizer, and the act of organization – everything is the same –* as we will see later on.

Summing up, consciousness is the lowest – or smallest – level of reality humans have a relationship with. That relationship is order and manifests as an order. Were we physically relative to that field, we wouldn't experience it as consciousness. In a way, our physical realm of observation could probably be some other observer's field of consciousness. The universe is most definitely conditioned by the same boundaries that limit us, so our reality is the result of such a condition. We are not exempt from the constraints that total disintegration presents. Therefore, as time builds reality, layer by layer, it made us; in doing so, we are constantly seeking to adapt, in the most symmetrically possible way, to it. However, psychologically, we gave it a structure that is fragmented and incomplete. As we previously saw, all kind of relationship problems arose from that fragmentation of time into past, present, and future. Since to observe is to die, death is what ultimately needed and created the framework of time, mainly as an act of escape – like everything else we do.

The idea of the future was first: the baseline coordinate for the rest of our ideals. Since the idea of time already contains the future as one of its parts, time must have been the second ideal. The senses give us perception in the natural world, but consciousness gives us perception of its building blocks. Space and time, as they are naked, can only be seen by attending consciousness in actuality. No education degree, or high level of specialized knowledge, is required to do this. All human reality is the same. Consciousness can't stop to observe, but it can definitely provide the order to do so. To observe is the only feature of reality that is not a form of escape from conditioning. All of us, without exception, can see within and realize in observation all the answers to life's quest, including the matter of death.

Reality unfolds for all observers, as we set on a quest. Like a river, all quests are born out of the content of the fountain seeking to figure its way out. What we do for that content is to open the path through observation, so that it reaches the ocean we call knowledge. Nevertheless, what happens in the process is also what will happen in the end.

PART 2 – **GOD**

Chapter 3

IS GOD ACTUALLY SPACE?

"IN THE BEGINNING GOD CREATED THE HEAVEN AND EARTH.
AND THE EARTH WAS WITHOUT FORM AND EMPTY,
DARKNESS COVERED THE FACE OF THE DEEP..."
- *GEN 1:1-1:2*

In a spark of insight, humans thought of the hope a new day would bring. During a cold dark night, we imagined what gifts a new dawn might bring us. Just as we projected the idea of tomorrow, we must have projected what was making tomorrow possible as well. The idea of a new tomorrow was, and still is, the light in the dark, and we are surely grateful for the cause of it.

As an idea, God was born out of turmoil. After all, why would we need to inquire about anything if we were perceiving that everything was in its proper order? The human quest comes out of imbalances, and what we think is unjust. Even curiosity is a form of psychological imbalance. God was born out of the questioning of undesirable outcomes in reality. Many have said before that suffering brings us closer to God. Nevertheless, just like the word tomorrow, the word God became one of the most brutal means of exploiting other men.

All ideas are pure energy first, and the idea of God is no different. When that energy is applied unbalanced and irrationally, it serves as a weapon. When it is applied rationally, it acts as a means to strengthen relationships. Nevertheless, applied rationality in any form, not just in the form of some God, brings order.

If God exists, where is he? Well, as an idea, God lives in the future. If he was part of the past, it would mean he lives in our memories. Whatever experience we could have that might give us an idea of what God is, it would be just an illusion. All illusions are the forms that meaning – or our future – takes. For the majority of humans, God is our meaning, but we're just deceiving ourselves. We need to take God as an idea out of the picture. If God is the meaning of our lives, he is an idea, and as such he doesn't exist. On the other hand, we can cheat ourselves by thinking he's not an idea, that he is a fact, and so he really exists. The issue here is that whatever exists, whatever stands out in reality, in our field of perception, is defined. Definition is limitation. Then, he can only function over what has been delimited to be ideal, and not over everything. By that point he has become a mere deduction of actual or possible facts. God as either, ideal or fact, is a definition.

The exploiters of the concept of God, as a supreme being that really exists, are being irrational because "all things" are something. All things begin, and they end as well. But, let's say we buy into the idea that God is present in all things. Now, because all things are the parts of everything, we need to make something out of those parts. Do you see the problem? In regard to God, whatever we do, we end up in another abstraction, another deduction, another set of facts that need to be reduced in order to find meaning in them. Once we get that meaning, it's over. God has just become another disguised form of "tomorrow." To find meaning in God is to chase a flag that's always ahead, in the future. By definition, God neither exists nor does not exist. Like the present, God is totally different from reality.

One has a strong intuition that all things and their motion must have a cause. Our cause is time, but there must be an aspect of reality that's beyond it. We sense it as if it is within us, because at our center we actually see how it comes to life, so it's not just intuition. We are able to observe in actuality how insight brings new realities into existence. Earlier, I expressed that there's no science that can explain the jump: the reality leap that's between the fact and insight. We intuit that "the something" that's causing those new realities is the same something that's creating the gap between knowing and not knowing. The only issue is that the process lies beyond our understanding. *God is always one step ahead of us.*

Now, what is God? Why did he give qualities and properties to all the things in his creation? Why did he make everything in the first place? Why did he make suffering a part of human experience? Is it possible to ever experience God in life? Does one have to wait until one's death, or after time, to get to meet God? These and many other questions invade our minds when we contemplate the nature of God. Let's now explore the idea of God versus the actuality of God, and how that relates to our daily lives.

God is the Unknown and Manifests in the New

In general, our quest in regard to God almost always starts with a *"why?"* The reason for this is because *"why"* is judgement. For most of us, God is judgement. He is associated with good and evil, or right and wrong. We are rarely concerned with God himself, or with whether he has a nature or not. We spend our questioning effort assessing why things are the way they are. When we find answers to those questions, God is no longer. *"What is?"* is more important than *"Why God?"* If God is the cause of all things, we don't really need to know why. He is the why.

Before we go into the nature of God, we first need to see what our relationship is with the word *"God."* Our connection with God is the same one that we have with the word itself. Like space, or death, God (as a noun) is not more than a word. *Nothing defines God except for the letters in his name.* Although we usually accept the fact that God is undefinable, we still eagerly try to assess why he is undefinable. In doing so, we pose a framework, fooling ourselves into a new and expanded delimitation. Hence, to say he has no definition, and proceed to explain why, is the definition of one's idea of that undefined God.

Across all cultures, God is the word of man. Since our relationship with that word varies greatly depending on many social and cultural factors, we are not seeking any particular historical consequence, or to study him as if it were some branch of theology. Man has invented polytheism, monotheism, agnosticism, deism and atheism, among many other forms of theism. We aren't discussing any of them. No forms of social structures, nor institutionalized belief, is our focus of attention here. To call oneself an *"agnostic,"* *"existentialist,"* or a *"nihilist,"* one must first know where the word itself is coming from. The word always comes from the ideal, from the meaning we first give it.

To understand is a transformation, so to understand what's creating the word is more important than the shape and/or structure of utterances themselves. In learning what gives rise to all forms, there's a shift in the limits and meaning of words. Therefore, here we are only interested in the relationship at the level of one particular observer: oneself. Let's look at the word *"God"* as it is individually, and try to assess what relationship it bears to each of us. In its meaning, we could probably discover more about ourselves than about the superior being we have in mind.

To analyze the origins of the word from formal logic is fruitless, especially when trying to arrive to a collective consensus. For example, an interesting aspect of the root of the word *"God"* is evident in Romance languages. In most of them, the word God comes from the Latin *"Deus,"* which comes from the Proto-Indo-European root *"-dyu"* or *"-diew,"* which some scholars associate with *"daylight, light, or bright."* Some others associate it with *"heaven, sky,"* while others affirm *"Deus"* is just a mere adaptation of the word *"Zeus."* The Greeks had one version of it, the Romans and the Egyptians another; the inferences go on and on.

"God" is defined as *"supreme being."* We see etymologies vary greatly, as every culture has their own origin, depending on

their language. Nevertheless, most of them have one thing in common. At some point they relate the definition of the word with "*a spirit*" and/or with *life*. The word "*spirit*" comes from the Latin "*spiritus*", which means "*a breath,*" and also from the Proto-Indo-European "*-(s)peis*", which implies "*to blow.*" The variants of the word are many, but in most cases, it implies the "inflation and deflation," or "integration and disintegration" of things. For the majority of cultures, that's what God does. He is an integrator – or disintegrator – of reality.

Our connection with God is our relationship across space. We have always looked up to the sky. The heavens are vast, and through it the sun gives us the light of the life. The skies represent every possibility. At some point we thought to ourselves that if we can build a house on a piece of empty land, what could we build up there? What worlds might be awaiting us? We dreamt, and the stories were many. Some came up with the concept of eternity, and others with the idea of God – or many gods. The one thing we intrinsically understood was, and still is, that space is where all possible outcomes are present.

In the same manner, internally as we come to a complete halt and stay in total awareness, it is evident in our centers there is the exact same space we see up in the heavens. Is this coincidence? We set to work to figure that out. Two natural premises arise: we are filled with space at our very own center, and there is also space surrounding all of our skin. Noticing the possibilities before our eyes, we also see the same possibilities inside we observers ourselves. Humans' greatest power is the power to change ourselves and the conditions of the environment willingly. In learning, we change. Give a computer a new set of data, and it will expand its limits of computation.

Give humans new experiences, and we will seek to achieve more than what we could before. However, what we realized is that we don't really need new experiences to expand our limits, or to change. We saw that the same house we build outside was first built inside because the geometry came from within. A new idea, whether of the psychological order or physical form, is in essence a new aspect of reality.

The source of human creativity is our conditioner. We are what we are conditioned for. Therefore, even as an idea, God is a conditioner. The unknown brings about the quest, but out of the unknown the quest also ceases to be. Space is that unknown. Not even the atheist escapes this condition because for them God is nothing, and space is nothing. God is the source of human ingenuity; but, in seeking him, we come up with all sorts of distorted ideals, and even worse, we give power to those distortions. We set up orders of hierarchy, which represent in function our distorted version of the condition, and then we give it authority over the control of our social structure to procure collective security.

Order brings security, and that is the same as "to order." Order is an activity, which is perpetually secured; to order is to set limits inside the whole of the observed. The direction, which is the result of ordering, becomes an asymmetry in relationship to the rest because of scale (as it was discussed earlier.) Thus, the idea of security comes from our perception of order, and it conditions us heavily. Security is a function of what we call death, and that's why only the present is sure. God resides in the present, and he manifests in the quality of what is.

The idea that God is right in front of us and everywhere – all the time – comes from the fact that he is what we don't know. So long as we remain ignorant of the hidden truth of our existence, there will be motion and a god from which all laws and answers are provided to us. Reality's design is so sketchy that one feels almost as if God is hiding in plain sight. It is like smelling a fresh but familiar aroma, which once we recognized, its magic disappears right away. God is the intelligence that arises when peace reigns. He is in the beauty of gratitude and silence. God is love and death, and he is always one dimension away from the observer.

The idea of God gives us purpose. There's nothing wrong with having a noble purpose, but we have to be aware that no purpose – in actuality – is real. I understand that we, as sane and well-functioning human beings, cannot possibly live without a vision. Thus, we cannot be without purpose. Again, the issue is that we refuse to accept that life's purpose is unobtainable because it lies outside of the edge of its margin. It is beyond all inferences. So long as we accept that fact, *we will find what God is.*

To understand the ultimate human conditioner is to see the unknown. From there, time reveals its real form, and truth starts to unfold.

God is not real, but it is true.

God's Touch is not Linear

By now we should be conscious of the effects that our perception of time has over pretty much everything else there is to perceive. Symmetry is time's primary goal because that secures its perpetuity. However, over ts span, as the angle of the observer changes, it becomes distorted. Since symmetry is relative to the position of the observer in the field, what might initially seem like a distortion in direction, could just be part of a more rational structure in the larger or smaller picture.

In that regard, the role of space is crucial because what we are calling "relative" is completely determ ned by the "spread" of the relationships inside a given framework. In turn, the framework itself becomes disordered or ordered, depending also on the space that relates it to multiple other frameworks. In other words, space determines what is true and what is false for all observers. *What is true is the becoming of time, what is false disintegrates.*

Space makes up that which has parts. As long as there are at least two parts there is observation and perception, and that's why we're so sure there is not one single unobservable point in the entirety of existence. The universe is made of infinite parts, and that *which is* only *is* what it is because of the observer's scope. In a way, the universe is empty if we say every observable point in it is space before anything else. There are two main reasons that might help explain why the design is such: on the one hand, space allows for function, or it is itself the functioning; on the other, without space we wouldn't perceive how it functions. Under the previous premises there is no need to distinguish between space, function, and observation. To do so would just serve to give us perspective, and the danger of it are the illusions of time.

When there's a misunderstanding of the statement that God is omnipresent, it usually is because of the importance we place on facts. Experience gives us facts, and that places us where we are today. The problem with the concept of presence – as something one experiences – is that it's not until time comes into effect that God would manifest. At that point, he is just another of our illusions. God's touch is not linear because not knowing is absolute in nature, and that is proportional to all other things – in principle. There's not knowing, and that gives us the order in the things known. Our current understanding tells us that one seeks the other, but in truth not knowing is what constitutes all the parts of the things we know. Even though order doesn't seek any specific outcome, an extraordinarily beautiful geometry is the outcome. Order simply acts by manifesting harmony or dissonance in perception. We see it working every time we stop and attend. When we align thought to what consciousness is telling us, we see how proportional and just our decisions become.

Our need to give God a definition or a framework comes from our perception of progressiveness. Our understanding of judgment in a linear manner can't be without progression. In a moral sense, God's judgement manifests as the false transitioning to that which is true. False is associated with wrong, and that is not true. Indeed "truth" is right, and "falsehood" is wrong. Nevertheless, for the outcome of decision making, what's *true* is not always right, and *false* is not necessarily wrong. As per each observer, it is usually the case that one feels compelled to displace what is wrong – or not ideal – to progress ahead to what is right. We eliminate what's false, and in its death the truth arises. Similarly, and ideally, the death of the wrong of the world is supposed to give rise to the right. Nevertheless, the whole business is just another play on our idea of time shaping the perception of reality.

For example, take a terrible illness. As bad as it is, in our world it is true that awful circumstances inhabit the lives of many humans. Still, the part God has in this is that of being true or false in the direction of the fact. In his role, God has no nature in the eyes of the observer. In all directions, nature is not. There is a distortion in the way we picture the creator for the sake of specific human agendas, but our hint of such a higher power in us is our ability to take turns and choose to go in other directions.

To conclude, since God has no proportions, it is only in observation that he manifests. Without dimensions, it is not possible to measure, and with the impossibility of measurement, the best we can do is make the word God. The reference of the word will always exist as long as there is an observer. The act of observation, which is a quest, produces an answer. The shape of such an answer is the reference onto which we cling to navigate this plane. However, all references are in relationship because of space, and that space is the center, or the observer himself.

God looks a lot like two empty centers separated by a limit.

PART 3 – **THE PROMISE OF A CHANGE**

Chapter 4

HUMAN CONDITION

THE CONDITION CREATES THE IDEAL.
THE HUMAN IDEAL IS TO CHANGE THE CONDITION.

To live is to be conditioned. There isn't a way to exist and not be shaped by the external. In order to *stand out* in the outer world, all living beings have to fit in relationship to that which is giving them life. Like a puzzle, life has to adapt to the forms of reality, and in doing so it limits itself to the specific forms that it surrounds itself with. As life makes its way through existence, it finds a series of limitations. One of the main obstacles it faces is the question of what its sources of energy are, and how much it is able to move to get to that source. A tree doesn't need to move because it feeds on sunlight, water and air. A tiger, on the other hand, needs to hunt other animals, so it moves a lot. For life to thrive, energy consumption should at least be equalized to energy expenditure. It is precisely energy availability that makes their movement possible. Therefore, as the origins of energy vary, organisms have to find new strategies to keep on finding it.

Life's purpose is to expand its own limits. Inanimate objects can't do this by their own means, but life is different. Since life observes, it seeks the spaces where there are no limits. Life realizes that there are gaps to be filled because there's discontinuity, which is exactly where observation lies.

Observation is not where space is filled. Instead, where the structure of reality is the weakest, space is abundant in relationship to the rest of the parts. Life's greatest achievement is to see that space. The fittest is the one who best adapts, and that is only possible for those able and willing to change. Change is the function of space, and there is no need to distinguish that from observation. From the emptiness, which is the possibility, an organism determines where the best outcome fits, and so long as it keeps doing so, it will continually find energy to thrive.

The probabilities which take place in space lead to the emergence of mutations that allow organisms the expansion of internal devices, or the creation of new ones to access new fields of perception in reality (e.g., a new sense.) The best answer science provides for such changes is that it is a random event. However, it seems that the very thing that's been kept hidden from us is the same thing that creates such mutations. Observation is driving these changes in living creatures. Life is a self-integrating or self-dividing system dependent on its environment, and in its activity, it eventually led to us.

Humans are the form of time. Through its guidance, consciousness gave rise to a higher order of expansion. In us, life went much further, as we broke the barrier of our physical body and its senses by creating the external devices we call technology. In the human body, consciousness has found a device which let it extend its reach to the outer world more rapidly and effectively than any other creature on the planet. However, humans are a work in progress because the work of time never stops. It's not where are we going to end up that matters, but to not end up at all.

In defining our condition, many men have come up with all sorts of ideas. Primarily, when it comes to humanity, we are mostly concerned with happiness. The single most highlighted aspect of the human condition across most sociological and cultural disciplines is happiness. Why is it not energy or logistics? Does energy have anything to do with happiness? Humans happen to be the only creature on this planet that feeds themselves with dreams. No other animal gets energy from ideas. For us, happiness is the pinnacle of all the justifications for the pursuit of the ideal.

When one is happy, one is full of energy. Happiness doesn't need any food, or shelter, or even health. If one is healthy, one is happy of course. However, independently of one's condition, one is happy when events turn out well. The word happiness comes from the root *"hap,"* which means *"good fortune."* Happiness is associated with security, and is a synonym of content. The word *"content"* comes from the Latin word *"contentus,"* which means *"satisfied."* *"Contentus"* is formed by the Latin root *"com-,"* which means *"with, together,"* and *"tenere,"* which means *"to hold."* In essence, content means *"to hold together."* If we remember the meaning and roots of the word knowledge, which I previously discussed, a pattern starts to emerge. To *"comprehend"* comes from the Latin *"comprehendere,"* which means *"to take together."*

Happiness is contentment; now, w*hat is the contentment of man*? The contentment of man is his content, and that is what he comprehends. *Happiness is when man comprehends.* To be happy, man has to know, but what does he have to know? Well, I pointed out that knowledge is the lim t between what is and what is not. Knowledge is time. Man's content is the content of time, which initially is the limit of thought. Thought breaks its own barriers through the word. It is in the word that man finds what's true or what's false. That which is true is never a limit, so as long as direction is true, time has continuity. In that which is false there's always a limit, and that's where man as a creature finds himself.

Let's not take the previous metaphor lightly. In his attempt to adapt to the conditions of life, man saw a way through the invention of abstractions he could test in reality. Even though *"tomorrow"* doesn't exist, the word says *"there will be a new dawn,"* and indeed, man sees the proof of the word in a new dawn. Many weaponized that tool out of fear, and others made it their source of security. While some saw chaos in the future, others saw great opportunities. Just as life emerged from the oceans millions of years ago to become today's Homo sapiens, time emerged from a sea of consciousness to become the word of humans.

When man was finally able to stop and stand up in front of the mirror of himself, he realized his condition was time. Our creator bargained life and gave us the power to do as we please, under one single condition. We can laugh or cry, love or suffer, make poetry, harm others or even ourselves (as horrible as that is.) However, the one thing that's not negotiable is death. The universe made us so that we are bounded, in abstraction, and in perpetual relationship. So long as the relationship exists, we exist.

But, what does it mean to die? What is death? Is death just another word we invented for something we have not even the remotest idea of how to define? These, and more questions surrounding the end, have been the most fundamental human dilemmas. *To live, we have to die – why?* Finding the meaning of death is just like finding the meaning of God. When one gets it, it is already too late. Nevertheless, there's at least one reference from which we can dive into that matter. In regards to finding meaning in death, we always arrive at the furthest point of whatever idea of the future we could have. Meaning, *the furthest point known to man in the future is death*. We at least have that, and we consider it to be truth. The implications become immediately worrisome because, as an idea, death has terrible applications in human thought. If the idea of the future is our best invention, death is our worst.

In other people and organisms, we witness death as total disintegration, but one cannot ever get to know what that means oneself because no one has returned from death to give us insight about it. Religions claim some have died and been resurrected, but even if we share the idea, to die and come back is just resurrection, not death itself. The story of a resurrected man is not the story of a dead man. The idea of death has brought most of the destruction we have seen in the world, yet the ultimate purpose of man is to die.

Purpose is objective. The word *"purpose"* comes from the Latin *"propositum,"* and it is composed by the Latin prefix *"pro-,"* which means *"in front of,"* and *"positum,"* which means *"to put."* Thus, purpose means *"that which is put forth,"* and the thing that's always put forth is tomorrow. *The ultimate tomorrow is always the last before death*. Under purpose we invent all kinds of deceptive statements "Tomorrow, I'll do it," "tomorrow, I'll stop," "tomorrow, I shall change," and the most infamous one, *"when I die."* In observing one day in our lives, we don't see much progression. Nevertheless, if we zoom out a couple of years, a pattern starts to emerge. That is, progression is the seeing of both the beginning and the end. With the ending in mind, one sees if there's actually progress. Therefore, progression is the beginning becoming the end. *The progress of our lives is the becoming of death.*

Becoming is the pursuit of time, so progression in thought is a serious issue. As individuals, as families, as countries, as religions, etc., there's becoming because thought sees the end, and it seeks to go in that direction. In consciousness there's no progression. Consciousness' exclusive concern is order, and besides giving rise to direction, it has absolutely nothing to do with it once it takes a path. By, "taking a path," I mean the becoming of order into thought. Direction needs an order, but the order doesn't control direction. *Order is not control.*

In the space between order and reality we hope to have a measure so that we can program our machines and our inventions to gain more control. We think that by having more control we are going to be more secure. It's all mere ideas. Even if we can have the content of that space, there would always be an extent to life, and from that there is no escape. We fool ourselves there's a place – a dimension – where the escape lies. There's no escape. As long as we see that fact in present time, we will meet what death is before we progress to the ideal of it.

The idea of death breeds our need to escape, and such a need is felt as fear. Fear is one of the many forms the future takes. That's what the whole of fear is: simply a vision into an undesired happening. In the present, fear is only a feeling. Fear is the peak of all dissonances in consciousness. Fear itself is not a bad thing, as it is consciousness telling us that something is off. However, when fear becomes a delusion, it puts us into a pathetic emotional state because it is each one of us who are giving it strength. Therefore, it makes us seek outside agency from our own selves.

Our reality becomes twisted when the form the escape takes grows in just one direction. As order fades, visions of death become inevitable, and fear becomes stronger, and so on. When one stays in the present, in observation, fear ceases to exist. The present is whole; it is pure order. Only in the future one becomes; in the present one only dies. The human condition is to die, and that is to live.

A Savior that Will Never Come

As we see, the human condition leads to all kinds of conflicts. We dream to keep ourselves away from the truth, but we also know it doesn't matter how big the dream is; there's no way out. In the invention of tomorrow, hope was born. Since hope is hard to sustain, we came up with faith. Hope is the image, the goal. Faith is a feeling in present time generated by the image of that goal. The way it works is by means of desire. Faith is like the stubborn version of desire. Desire comes from the past in the form of the future. We already saw where it leads. All illusions lead to delusion, which then turn into disappointment, and finally frustration. Violence emerges from all of that. Violence is resistance against direction. In seeking a direction, insecurity is bred. When the order of the word fails, time acts as energy. This is why, in practice, law and order are ultimately kept by force.

Order in the sense of a command is not different to order as a noun. Hence, *one orders, and security is built-in in that order*. To say one is sure – without the ordering – is to say one has faith. To be certain without any specific order is what we call "to believe." The observer sees there is no particular direction that leads to an outcome, and he hopes out of faith the future will unfold just as he hoped for. It's not such a big deal, but it is just gambling.

Now, what happens when we place hope in others? That is, what happens when our understanding limits order, and we place the responsibility on the shoulders of another? This situation is much worse – if not the worst – and it's precisely what we have been doing since the beginning of civilization. Simply put, to have faith is to say one doesn't know. What's wrong with that? As I exposed, happiness comes from knowledge. See the pattern? One is not happy, so one hopes there will appear someone who does know.

Since joy comes from within, it can't be sold, but happiness can. Leaders come and go, promising happiness. Most of our economic and political theories are based on the idea that governments must secure the happiness of the people. Supposedly, happiness will arise from security. This is not true. Security is not provided; security is, or is not. Progress leads to happiness, but not necessarily to order. Thus, progression can't lead to security.

Why do we seek to be provided with security then? As if it was some kind of commodity, we expect an external and greater power to grant it to us; but why? The answer is that we have been conditioned that way. In previous chapters, I commented about a ancient person seeing the abstraction of what *meaning* really is, and when out of it a new order emerged, we just kept replicating it. The shape of the order changes. Empires, religions, communism, capitalism, etc.: they are some of the many forms that every new order takes. However, time hasn't changed, not even a bit. The one idea that has remained completely intact since its inception, is the idea of time. Therefore, we haven't really changed anything. *We have had the same order since our time began.*

How do we expect for things to change if the order is the same? One orders, and this ordering produces an outcome. The order of our society was given long ago, and that is the provider of our security. To us, modern humans, security is something to attain. Our leaders say, "you will be secured," but *only death is sure, so time is the order* – evidently. Why is it so hard to see it? We study one idea after another, and another, and so on. Theories after theories, chasing our tails. The outcome will always be the same because the order is the same. I don't think the solution is in anything that could be applicable or in the practice. Unless we change, internally like a mutation, things will continue in the same way.

The first thing to do in this regard is to assume complete responsibility over one's own existence. One has to recognize there is no savior. Whatever observation is, it doesn't need outside agency. Thus, no one will come to show us a way out of our condition. We are dying; that is inevitable. In seeing that, we open the path for new possibilities. Individually, we create the space for novelty. In assuming responsibility for one's own life, as big as it is, the creative mind arises, and all knowledge becomes available. Life opening its way through reality is space. Intelligence is the reading of such space, so how is one to see those gaps while expecting another to provide it? *Space cannot be provided; It just is there, in the pause*. The observer is in motion when he lives in the present. When we are caught in our desires, we are caught in the future. To be free of that is to have no need for a savior.

Time Travel:
The Most Sophisticated Fairy Tale Ever Told

Among all the fantasies we wish to make reality, no other is more dreamt of than time travel. Since we came up with the concept of time, we have imagined what it would be like to "go back" to change the past, or "go forward" to alter the future. Our advances in the comprehension of physics have led to the fueling of this old dream of ours to alter reality by changing the course of events outside the present. We saw that our condition feeds itself by devising escapes, and the form the escape takes is always the next happening, which is the condition itself. Put another way, the thing invents itself, and then tries to escape what it invents.

To start off, where does the perception that time only goes in one direction come from? It comes from the fact that events can't be undone. If we slam a glass of water against the floor, not only will the glass break, but the water inside will be spilled. Putting all the shattered pieces back together again will be a seemingly impossible task, not to mention putting all the water back inside the glass as well. Physicists call this property of reality entropy. We are not going to delve into all of the details of what entropy is. However, for the sake of context, it is a property of the universe to move from order to disorder. Entropy as a concept is very real, but beside the physical limitations it presents, it doesn't seem to have anything to do with the direction of time. Indeed, reality does move in a specific direction; however, there is an opposition to such direction – otherwise we wouldn't perceive such movement as direction in the first place. That which opposes motion in a particular path is what we call force. A force is a limit. It is a hint that time is not merely a push forward. In fact, aligned to what has been previously proposed, it seems that time is resistance to all other non-mechanical movements, so that it leaves the perception of only one way instead.

Once more, to think of rewinding events back in reality, as if we were in a movie playing on a screen, is just an interesting story. Still, matter and energy are frequently collapsing, and in consciousness one sees that the layers they build move back and forth. In reality, it's fair to say that we receive as much as we give, but the version of time humans invented is something that takes but doesn't give back. Again, without the intention to fool ourselves, what has been done cannot be undone, that is clear. What is not clear is what that has to do with the direction of events other than giving the observer a framework or the image of a reference.

Let us put it this way: if no one ever dies, why would anyone want to go back in time? Say one is eternal, why change anything? If one doesn't die, then whatever situation will pass, one will still be here. However heartbroken we are, in time we could endlessly try to repair it. The idea of time travel is one of our great escapes. It's a nice try, but it is not enough.

Now, why would anyone want to change the future? Before we continue with this fantasy, let's pretend that the future is certain, that it is some destination, so it truly exists. First, if a future outcome is certain, it is because of the order of things. It was previously assessed, there's no need to distinguish order from security because they're both the present in action. Therefore, certainty is order in the making, and that will result in a future outcome, which will follow through the same order. Why not change the present then? Why waste energy on all this nonsense, and simply take action in the present?

Now, suppose whatever action we take in the present will inevitably lead to a vision of some future. For example, let's take death. As I mentioned earlier, we don't know what death is. We know the body disintegrates, but we don't know what that word really means. Death is right after meaning. It's not as simple as to say that we don't know how to change the outcome of death, but that the outcome itself is an unknown, so no order can be given to it. *What is not known in the present is not different in essence than what we call future.* There's nothing to change by "traveling to the future" because there's literally "no thing" in our content in that direction. Meaning, if the destination is an unknown, what coordinates do we program our "time travel device" to take us to? Death is inevitable because there's no knowledge which can prevent it from happening, so we are living. Say one doesn't die, is one alive then?

The present is alive. To the mind, the present is perfect because it contains the whole of reality without any psychological fragmentation. If there really was a Big Bang at the beginning, we are still that Big Bang. It didn't happen; it is still happening. At the base of the universe there's a function, and since it cannot be interrupted, that is an abstraction to us. Unlike time, the flow of space cannot be interrupted because there cannot be fixed points inside that which is infinite. In the same manner, there can't be infinite points inside a finite universe. Existence is an abstraction because we are an open system changing constantly through a present state. The universe, which is that same abstracted existence itself, must be an open system too. It is infinite in all directions and at every point – not just infinite from beginning to end. Each observed point is infinite.

To fix the path of time, as a forward progression inside a framework, limits us to merely mechanical achievements. It really looks as if it were an error. It is a problematic perception, and I think it needs to be fixed. Life for humans, as it is today, has the right psychological conditions for a new framework of reality. One which could take us anywhere without so many interpersonal imbalances and logistical constraints.

As for relationships between humans, it is easier to fantasize about changing one's actions to avoid undesired or horrendous events in the past, instead of taking action in the present. We ourselves contain the whole of the past; why not change it now? I don't necessarily have the whole of the answer to such a question, but I'm raising the flag to simply say that's what we are. It is change that we are concerned with, not time. Can the facts and possibilities both be met in the present? If one really faces them, with deep observation, the unknown reveals the real structure of time. Of course, there are random externalities; events one regrets. There are experiences that are beyond our control – but as long as one is alive, one has the power to change the past through the present. In living, we already know what the future will look like.

Modern Times:
Human Intelligence vs Artificial Intelligence

Another one of those inventions that fuels the machinery of our modern fears is that of artificial intelligence. Robots taking over humanity has been a latent concern ever since we made them capable of automatic processes. This section aim is not to discuss the history and/or mechanics of machines and/or computers. In turn, let's analyze what our relationship with these marvels of human invention is, and why we shouldn't fear them.

Before anything, we need to distinguish what is human, and what is artificial. Then, let's recall what intelligence is. In the context of the word "intelligence," both "human" and "artificial" are being used as adjectives, not as nouns. The relevance of this, in this modern debate of ours, is that human and artificial are qualities of the word intelligence. We know quality is a stablished by space. Both the spread of space and the speed of that space changing limits is what provides "human" and "artificial" the starting point of comparison in reference to the reach of that intelligence. Therefore, to be congruent with the definition of intelligence, I'm inferring that the scale across space that humans and machines observe, and the speed at which such a scale changes, determines the scope of intelligence in each one. Let's remember, every point of observation in the universe is a center, and it is infinitely empty until time emerges from it. We call that process intelligence.

The word "intelligent" is an adjective used to qualify the measure of an outcome or performance. When discussing this topic, we assume that humans are intelligent, and that machines are intelligent as well – meaning that they both produce a qualifiable outcome. Let's figure out what it is to be human, what is artificial, and whether all outcomes from performance are really a measure of intelligence.

I previously discussed intelligence, but let's refresh our understanding of the concept. "Intelligence" comes from the Latin "*intelligere*." It is composed by the Latin "*inter-*," which means "*in between*," and "*legere*," which means "*to read*." Since intelligence is one's ability to "*read in between*," we'll assume that the ability to produce a qualifiable outcome is reciprocal to the accuracy of the seeing of relationships in space. However, an inconvenience arises from measuring intelligence merely by the quality of outcome because part of it is also the quality of the function creating such results. For example, how can we measure the psychological function of a human?

Let's recall that function is abstraction, abstraction is the future, and the furthest point in the future of man is his death. How are we to measure death if it doesn't have any reference? Until we are able to measure what is to not know or space, there's no way we can measure intelligence.

Measurement can be qualified. The outcome of intelligence can be put into a coefficient, but not intelligence itself. Since we don't have a grip on intelligence, but only a reference after it took place, we tend to associate intelligence with computation. Computation is an important part of what intelligence is, but it lacks the most important component, which is observation. Observation itself can produce intelligent outcomes because it orders. Computation can only produce direction because it is the shape that the order adopts. That s, consciousness lets us know order, and the brain follows through by computing the order. In machines, that is not the case, as we'll see shortly.

It is very difficult to define what it means to be human. Nevertheless, for the purpose of simpl fying matters, we'll say humans are living organisms belonging to the Homo Sapiens species. As a living organism, we are separated from inanimate matter because all life can tell and sense time. As Homo sapiens, we stand apart from the rest of the animal kingdom mainly because we can change time's direction faster than any other living creature. We can stop, observe, and have ideas that turn into abstractions. We make art, music, poetry, math, physics, chemistry, biology, etc. What really makes us humans different from the rest is intelligence. *We live in abstraction, creating and making art.*

That which is artificial is a copy. Our art is an abstract copy of our consciousness. An artifact is made so that it mimics some order. A man-made artifice contains a copy of a part of the human's psychological content. In that sense, an artificial "something" is the human attempt of that "something." Why would we need an artificial something? The issue really is not whether we need it or not, but rather to see that everything we make is artificial by straight definition. Ideas are natural, but their artifices are not. No human can create natural outcomes other than giving birth. Not even a clone, which is a biological copy, is natural because it is artificially or through a technique – copying DNA, and all the rest of it.

The word *"natural"* comes from the Latin *"naturalis,"* which means *"by birth;"* however, birth is still an act of replication. By definition, the birth of a living creature is the partial or complete copy of what gave birth to it. What is then the difference between a copy via birth and a copy via artifice or human technique? The difference between natural and artificial is content. The content of the artificial copy is not the same as the content of the natural. An artificial copy is a cheap version of the original. It is cheap because the content of nature is whole, whereas the content of the artificial is limited by thought. What thought creates contains a directing, so it is excluding a lot of the entire picture. If we say that artificial intelligence is going to outrun us, despite having less content than we do, then we are admitting that we are carrying too much.

Let's briefly come back to a previous topic, *"the content of man is what he comprehends,"* to improve the general context of what is meant here. Knowledge is the content of man. What he makes of a machine is the goal of knowledge towards the ideal function of such a machine. If the ideal is to get from New York to London in six hours, he makes the airplane in such a way as to make this possible. In this case, man thinks of a machine that could think faster than he does. In some regard, man himself wishes to compute information faster, and out of that ideal he creates artificial intelligence. There's only one little problem: computation is not intelligence.

We already have extremely fast computers, but that's not enough. Artificial intelligence is a deceiving story; it is just a much more complex and fancier attempt to keep death at bay. Man's greatest desire is not to create faster-computing beings, but to transfer consciousness through artificial means.

Consciousness is not transferable. Consciousness is a field common to all of existence, and it is dependent on the layer of reality where the observer lies. Consciousness says what's right and what's wrong, not by means of language or information, but by means of harmony in the relationship. Machines can't know harmony because harmony is in the silence, and silence can't be captured. We observed earlier that if we ever get to put our hands on consciousness, it would be worthless for the aforementioned objectives. Although consciousness is order, it can't get anywhere without thought. Ironically, thought can't reach everywhere either by itself because it needs order at its base. The "holy grail" of science, and the purpose of all human disciplines is to discover what connects the two.

We just don't know how order connects with direction. Initially, they look the same, but they're not. The reason why it seems we will never know the content of such a gap is that it is not in our field of perception. Consciousness is felt by us when it assists in structuring our abstractions, and the image it gives rise to is also in our perceptible reality. As per my human experience, I am completely certain that *the act of observation is what lies between consciousness and thought.* The funny thing about it is that observation and not-knowing are the same activity. I suggest that we can go deeper than consciousness, and I can see us achieving that. Nevertheless, it is an impossibility to go beyond observation, or beyond not knowing. The real and true action we should take is to expand the reach of awareness of humanity, but we can't do that by external means.

Externally, we don't perceive electromagnetic fields, for example, but we see them in action, so they are on a spectrum.

Whatever is on a spectrum, even if it is at the extreme end of it, can be abstracted. However, as I mentioned before, an abstraction only leads to more abstractions. In other words, the solution to an event that hasn't happened is an event that also hasn't happened.

Death is this thing which is outside of both our field of perception and time's structure. *Consciousness cannot create machines that die because thought doesn't know what that is.* Our creator made us capable of dying; yet, we can't copy it. *Death equals the idea.* Meaning, whatever an idea really is, it is not any different from whatever death also is. Machines can't have ideas because they can't die. Nature can create replicas with that capacity, but we don't. Sometimes, it seems as if we are hoping to learn from these machines what it means to live without the immensity of death. These machines can't teach us anything about death because they don't possess the means of deduction to understand – not even as a reference – what it means. There's nothing to abstract for them in that regard because it is not part of their content, nor the content of their creator. In a sense, since they're already dead, they can't know what living is either. Put another way, we don't know how to make machines capable of not knowing; therefore, we can't make them capable of dying. Machines don't have a real essence or notion of present time.

So, what does this all mean for us? We don't live mechanically. We live in abstraction and created machines that can't even see such an abstraction. These AI systems are not in any relationship, they don't know what time is. They know the version of time we program in them, but not the totality of it. How can destruction, if that's what we fear, be part of a thing that doesn't know what destruction is – really. *The problem is us, not the machine*. The issue with technology is not tech itself, but application. It has always been that way. When we applied "tomorrow" righteously, it gave us crops; however, when fear invaded us, we used it to bring about death.

Time pushes us to fill our empty centers since that promotes conservation. From the center applications come to life. This is called creativity. *Machines lack that center*. The emptiness in that center is the same emptiness we find in death. Our relationship with our creator is in that center. These machines' relationship with their creators – us – is not from an empty center at all. In fact, it is the opposite. Their relationship with us is totally filled. *Space for them doesn't exist because their knowledge is absolute.* Whatever we put inside, that's all that there's going to be between them and us. Even if such content can be scrambled into infinite forms, t will still be filled with noises from the past.

Our creator shows us the truth without giving us the tools to replicate it. In a sense, we hope these creations of ours could be our savior – but such a savior will never come.

Chapter 5

THE MEANING OF LIFE

LIFE IS A WONDERFUL THING.
NO THOUGHT CAN CATCH IT.
IT IS AS WHOLE AS DEATH.

Before all formal and institutionalized knowledge, humans had to find a way to explain to themselves what it meant for them to exist. There's nothing one can do; once one is alive, there's no turning back. In that, one is completely alone from birth to death, and out of despair one is compelled to find the meaning of that loneliness. It is such desire that creates the human quest. As extensively discussed before, the invention of the future, as the progression of time, couldn't have been born without the projection of some sort of goal in mind. That is, man visualizes himself reaching the top of a mountain, and from that he finds meaning, which is "tomorrow we'll get there." Meaning is not separate from abstraction, so meaning is abstraction. Since the edge of the future is an abstraction, it is our absolute meaning. Our main goal, before anything else, is always to make it to the furthest point in the framework.

Some us can't stand the idea of what the future will bring us, and from it we create all sorts of fantasies. We invented time travel in order to project the change in our fates. We invented quantum mechanics and particle accelerators to find a "God particle." We invented cloning and DNA manipulation to extend our lives. We invented computers and artificial intelligence systems to attempt the transfer of consciousness. We lead compulsive lives because we favor the escapes that provide the fastest relief. Such compulsions eventually lead to addictions, which in turn convert into a fast track to self-annihilation (or death). Compulsions and addictions are the most effective path to the mechanization of life. Ultimately, we have invented careers, family, society, economic systems, philosophy, religions, God and his many saviors.

Why have we invented so many forms of escape, and made them our purpose? Why is it that humans can't stand this life without an ideal purpose?

There's no doubt about it, just as we walk and talk, we have to have meaning. It is just as part of what we are as our pair of hands. Our life is an abstraction because death is also an abstraction. We live running from an "invisible monster" that has never shown its face. We know death's work not because of rotten bodies, but because of the way we live. Death's work is not on a spectrum since it is itself the entire spectrum. Although we don't see it directly, we know that it shows the whole array of meaning. It is very simple: *to abstract reality is to die.* The living meets the unknown, and calls it death.

If death is the ultimate purpose, the real question we have to put to the test is, can death ever be met? I'm not talking about the atrocities humanity has made in the name of some meaning. To finish a life is not to meet death; that would be to physically fade away, and the two are not the same. The loss of integrity of the systems inside the human body in a chain reaction is a portion of death, but it is not the whole of it.

There's a section of the entire picture that happens now, during the living part of our existence. Can we get to know what it is? If death could be faced during one's life — if that is possible — there wouldn't be any need to wait until the body is tired, and ceases to be, to know what "meaning" means. Let's figure out whether the final goal of life can be met before the end of one's existence, and what it would signify for us.

Art and Beauty

All the forms that human activity takes are an act of imitation. Our work is a replica of our psychological content, and that content is a replica of time. In principle, such an act of replication is not an act of our will. Time has its hands on everything in the universe. At this point you are probably aware that there's no use in splitting psychological time from its activity of the physical world. If we agree time is the relationship between an initial limit and a final one, with multiple progressions of sub-relationships inside it, then a limit in a thought is the same limit as the limit of a "chair" that one is seeing in reality. The limit in the thought of the chair is the initial one and the color of wood in the actual chair could be the final one. The function is everything that could or will happen in between, until the last – conceptual or physical – possibility of the chair is met.

This perception of the property of progression is how we make sense of time. A good metaphor for it when acting in the present would be to think of time as a rock and space as the wind. Moment by moment, the wind erodes the rock, just as space, moment by moment, "erodes" the structure of time.

We replicate ourselves via birth, we plant trees and flowers, we draw, we make sculptures, we make robotic arms, we smash atoms, we make intelligent machines, and so on. It is all the work of time giving direction by attempting to multiply itself. All human activity, except for biological functions, is copied from nature. However, even biological functions are modified versions of the function of the previous part (or parts) responsible for it, which was also copied through time. Humans are perpetually in an act of imitation. We refer to this act of replication by many names, depending on how we want to be perceived by others. We are mirroring in a mechanical way what nature is already doing, and every time our craft leads to success, we keep on crafting to repeat the success over and over again. The inference is that if everything we make is artificial, then it is all art. However, art as mere imitation of the external is just a form of entertainment.

Replicating forms is not art; it is entertainment. Skill is entertainment. Skill is technique and method. From technique comes technology. The definition of the object is the definition of the technique. Art in the object makes the artifice, so art as the result of skills is that which is artificial. In the name of art, we make artificial flowers, an artificial sculpture of a person, and so on. When beholding art is entertaining, there is a superficial relationship between the observer and the past, so an ideal begins to spark. Art as entertainment is pleasure.

Pleasure is always a moment ahead. Entertainment is when the idea of the next thing is in sight, and one seeks a way of passing time while that 'next' exists in reality. Pleasure is the artificial form that joy takes, so we can't possibly obtain gratitude from it. *Gratitude leads to the highest forms of art.* In gratitude, beauty is at work. Without gratitude there's no passion, and without passion there's no love. There is no difference between absolute gratitude and love. They're both the same, and they lead to art from insight, which is the best art.

At the beginning of the book, I talked about peace. There can't be gratitude without peace. Peace is a quality of perception.

From there, one can abandon all intentions because fear and the condition disappear. Paradoxically, if we bring the condition to an end, it would mean the death of time. Death doesn't bring death to itself, but it does bring death to time. Can time end, and death still be a thing? I don't think death is a condition brought up by time. One is an 'orange,' the other is an 'apple.'

Art from insight, which is the making of the original, is not an escape from our condition, but rather the direct work of it. We don't make music or poetry to live longer. The music we dance to is entertainment, but the making of the music and the dancing are not. The poetry we read to a loved one is entertainment, the passion we feel when we are writing the poem is not. Still, we don't pay attention to the dance, nor to love, because we always seem to have something (ahead) in mind.

When art has an agenda, it is not art – it is business. Business in the sense of occupation. The word "business" is composed by "*busy*," which is occupied, and the suffix "*-ness*" signaling quality. Later on, business was split from busyness to differentiate commercial activity from occupation. In essence, business literally means the quality of an occupation. *Everything we do that is not creative is business.* We seek business to fill and occupy our centers. In the first chapter, I talked about what space is, and how its emptiness is where peace, gratitude, and beauty reside. The bright red of a rose is determined by the vibration level of the light in the visible spectrum, and that is determined by the spread of space in between the peaks of each wave of vibration.

Now, if space gives us beauty because of quality, it must also give us ugliness. Death is where nothing is. In a sense, what gives beauty its quality is the same thing that is the ugliest of all. The artist has to live with these two facts in order to make art. In facing the nature of the quality of beauty, there's no need for measurement. Beauty is a symmetry in the relationship, which is a state of harmony. For example, we know light gives us colors. Earth's favorite colors are blue and green, both of which are in the middle of the visible spectrum. Green is a very symmetrical color. Alternatively, red, which is at the very end of the spectrum, represents death for most of us. Harmony in a relationship determines which limits survive in time and which don't.

To live an artistic life is to live a life that offers more liberty from the turmoil of this world. What this means is that we live with death, rather than running away from it. Metaphorically speaking, we let it work because it is trying to show us better ways out. We seek to hold reality all together, but reality is vulnerable to the immensity of space. Therefore, we split more and more, continuously, until we are no longer. A true artist works side by side with the ruler of the universe. Great art arises when the living is in harmony with what gave it emergence, but that never happens tomorrow or yesterday. It is clear that art from yesterday is entertainment, and the art of tomorrow has an agenda. *The present is the artist, and the artist is one with the art.*

When art comes from will, it's a subtle form of violence against oneself and aggression against others. Imitation is competition. To imitate in a better fashion is to be competent, and out of competition there can't be art. Whatever we force ourselves to

130

do is part of an agenda, not art. When one says, "I must finish this work," or "I will continue tomorrow," etc., there is strictly a process of imitation. The mind sees an objective, which is other than art, and one forces the body to craft art as a medium to achieve such purpose. There's nothing wrong with making an effort, but it is of the utmost importance to know what process is really going on. If one is after money, fame, achievement, status, etc., then the resulting work is not really a creative one. I am not saying that whoever is after such goals shouldn't pursue them, but I'm stating that the result of that can't possibly be great art.

Now, there's a way to lead an artistic life independently of the activity, and it can be achieved through awareness. When the seeing of the process is the main part of the process, creativity comes to life. Art that doesn't come out of will, out of competition, or the need for fame and money, is the result of deep conscious levels of attention. True art is the art of living a creative life.

One notices that, when the work is completely passionate, it does itself. Why? It seems someone else is making the work when one turns oneself completely to the present moment and is one with the work. In passion, the perception of time disappears.

Understanding our limits allows us to see what lies beyond, and in parallel art takes place. In the art-making process, even being aware that what lies beyond is always a new limit, consciousness allows us to look in different directions. Awareness really gives us scales of dimensions that we couldn't possibly have gotten without art. Nevertheless, if we continue in the way we're doing now, we'll become biologically unable to detect that field. We'll be too dependent on our artifices, and our lives will become too artificial and mechanical. Just as we got access to the field of consciousness, we might as well lose it.

At the precise moment of making art, consciousness can't be twisted or perverted. Therefore, we need to incentivize true art, so our relationship with the field of consciousness is kept alive. The artist is a diligent listener. All of us are the artists of this earth. However, the less we listen to the voice of the universal law giver, the farther away we are from our greatest power, which is the power to change "*what is.*" Through artistic means, it is possible to meet our center, *while living.* We don't know where this might lead us, but through a passionate life, we could change the conditioner's mind.

Change

The universe exists, then humans exist.
Humans are born out of the universe.
The universe is conditioned; therefore, humans inherit its condition.
To know the primary condition of one man is to know the primary condition of humanity.
To know the condition of one man is necessary to observe psychological processes.
The aspects of the mind can only be looked upon one observer and one place at a time.
The observation of internal human processes can take place in seeing oneself within oneself.
Therefore, only in oneself can the primary condition of humanity be known.
In knowing of one's condition there's the meeting of it.
To be one with the condition is to be in harmony with life.
Through abstractions, the condition cannot be explained; yet, to abstract is our condition.
To abstract is to relate, so we live in relationship to the rest.
To explain the relationship is to create another relationship.
To see this condition is a unique human function.
Such function is observation.
Observation orders, but doesn't condit on.
Our greatest concern is to change humanity's condition.
Most of us hope that an external agent will bring such change.
However, only observation changes the condition.

At the level of our daily lives, there are two main aspects of humans' reality that drive the paths of human behavior. On the one hand, humans long for happiness, and in seeking happiness, we continually seek repeating pleasures. On the other, humans suffer because we find there's no relief in happiness for our condition. Through this work, it has been exposed that pleasure and happiness are really just one. Suffering is at the edge of all divisive activity. Death is the totality of both, suffering and happiness. I insist to be careful not to confuse what death is with the idea of death. I said that death itself is not really a condition. The line we draw at the end of all knowledge activity, and the membrane of what we imagine dying is, is the condition. In other words, our collective perception of time persuades us into calling the outermost layer of its framework 'death,' and we conclude that indeed that's the end.

All ideas are part of the structure of time, but death doesn't have a structure. A computer is not death, but it is the work of death. Or likewise, a rocket is not death, but it is the abstraction of death. Without death, creativity doesn't exist. Reading this work, you might have evaluated the many fight-or-flight responses that death produces, and you probably saw that these encompass the whole of human activity. Although we are determined to change our fate, we inevitably try to deal with pain through pleasure, not being aware that the pursuit of pleasure only fuels the condition. Pleasure by itself is not harmful. Since one has a physical body, even against one's will, one is exposed to stimuli. As I exposed before, things really complicate when the repetition of pleasure becomes compulsive. Addiction, which is the most extreme form of compulsiveness, is not a problem of society initially, but of the individual. By not seeking awareness of their own existence – out of despair and misery – humans get trapped in a compulsive state of uncontrollable repetition. It is from such a state that we want to be freed, and it is not only drugs or other vices we wish to have autonomy from, but mostly from our daily and mechanical lives. The shift from despair to bitterness is a thin line, and as our lives become more mechanical, fear and anger grow like an uncontrollable fire. Pleasure becomes like the wind that instead of extinguishing it, gives it power, and facilitates such transition.

God made us, and did so that we are in perpetual pursuit. Now, in that statement, we find a different quality to living. In such a statement, there's a quest, which is the question of what it is that we are pursuing. The funny thing is, in questioning what are we seeking, we just began another pursuit. From the unknowingness, all of us inquire. The best way to lay the foundations for any debate, of any nature, is to start off by seeing our inexistence. Death is an infinite source of compassion. God made us all equal in that regard so that, from there, pride didn't invade our lives. From ideas, pride can shield us, but from the unknown we are all naked, face to face with one another.

Knowledge is happiness, but it is also pride. Pride is the fancy costume of resentment. It is a disguised form of bitterness, which is why having authority makes us stubborn. In regard to our relationships, knowledge is our clothing, our colors, our nationalities, our genders, and it is our many reasons. We take pride in whatever we identify with, but it is impossible to see each other as equal if the measure of our relationships comes from our psychological identities. When we agree to start a discussion from the observation of our centers, acknowledging that we are actually dying, the psychological structure of time is destroyed, meaning that hate, jealousy, envy, anger, pride, and all desires get destroyed. As we evolve in such dialogue, it will be clear that things take a specific direction anyway, but at least we'll be progressing side by side along the way. At whichever point we split in reasoning, we can always come back to the center and realign the ideas. From that, we can work much better – even with ourselves. Whatever conflict one has with oneself or with others, it gets resolved on that ground. *Space is the ultimate conflict-resolution aid.*

Deep down, we all want to change. We wish to not go to war, to not fight, to not be violent, to not yell, to not envy or desire what belongs to others. Ultimately, we wish not to die. It doesn't matter how or where we grew up; our strongest desire is to change. For one or another reason, there's constant inconformity in life, that's how we are: always on the move, seeking relief in a new day. Hope rests on the shoulders of faith as the image of change, but hope is always at the end of the spectrum – and we already know what that means. What time is best at is having us going in circles.

What is one to do?

The first thing is to strip yourself aside from all the psychological constructions imposed by your parents, school, government, society, etc. In a moment of introspection, you need to go deep within to your most basic essence. In such a regression, you'll inevitably realize that there are only three aspects to existence with which we construct our reality and its order. To the naked mind, there are: space, time, and motion. Although space is undefinable, we know it is there because it is the pause where we see all possible outcomes. Similarly, motion is also unmeasurable, but we can evidently see things moving. Time, out of the three, is the one that is a psychological construct. Therefore, at the base of every idea – without exception – lies the same mechanism which creates time. All ideas are a homologous with the future. If we want to change society and end most of our conflicts, we need to change our construction of time. In doing so, everything else will change. Even for the applicable realm, we could have a model that is entirely different, and thus one with completely different logistical implications. In changing the way time's structure conditions us, we will inevitably reform our logistical restrictions as well. We might even be able to set the foundations to create the right framework for time portals and solve the problem of large-scale distances.

Psychologically speaking, space and motion are absolute truths, but time – as it's now conceived – is false. Now, while humanity takes the big leap of changing the framework of time, is there a possibility to at least be psychologically and individually at peace with it? Let's see; space is before time, so before we even understand anything, we have to stop all thoughts not relative to what we consider time is, and observe the activity of consciousness. From such observation an order arises, and in such order there's a way to thought. The rest will follow through manifestations in the physical world. I think we have the capacity of creating whatever version of time we wish for, but the busyness of modern life alienates us from our true potential. I want to suggest that when you observe, try not to do so under the aim of application at first. Later in the thought process, application will rise anyway. In application there's necessarily purpose, and that is the road we are already walking on. Meaning, whatever new framework we come up with shouldn't be an ideal version of some end in the mind, but it rather be the result of the description of the actual aspect that was observed. It is necessary to think as abstractly as possible so that the quest leads to the observing of the observer himself. That is, don't stare at the unknown as a human observer, but as a center whose only function is to observe.

There is no difference in the orders of magnitude in observation. What we define as a function requires an order of magnitude, or a scale. Interestingly, life doesn't really need a scale to function. Humans make use of orders of magnitude for application, not to understand life. When the scale of the framework is too large, it becomes unmanageable. But, if we get rid of the framework, and its internal and external relationships, there's no use in splitting observation from our function. It is precisely what happens with time. Because we wanted to give it an application, we gave it a forward framework, and we now function according to it.

Our model of time can only serve mechanical means. Our machines adapt perfectly to this mechanistic approach to time because they have a specific end to serve. In fact, all of our mathematical advancements mostly serve our artificial toys. They apport very little to human relationships. Take gravity as an example. We don't need – in any way – to know what the effect of gravity is in order to knock a mango off a tree. We do need to know the extent of that effect to make our gadgets function according to a specific order. Whatever everything is, it's already built in for us to function without the need to abstract it.

Let's look at this: one observes the purple in an orchid. We know space gives it quality. One is aware that the space between the waves in the visible spectrum gives violet its color, and the distance between us and the flower gives the orchid its appearance. If we could have a reference or measurement for such a space, we would know exactly what the required framework is for an observer to see a purple orchid at any given time. Now, the question is, what for? Why would we want to know all of this? One sees a purple orchid, and that's it. Just as one doesn't need to calculate distance or speed to make a fruit fall from a tree, one doesn't need to have any formulations to see a purple orchid. Again, measurement only serves our artifacts. A machine doesn't see the purple orchid; we do.

Is it possible to observe the entirety of our lives in the same way that we look at the orchid? Can we look at each other without time, and without calculations? Without time there's no need to create an application for a function, and there's just observation. I suggested, should a framework be required for the sake of application, let it be, but it is not necessary for human relationships. Every time we apply a framework in human relationships, all we are doing is measuring each other. Human life, as it is, has no measure. One sees oneself, and in seeing one's limitations, one is caught in the entire composition of it. One is "this" or "that," and the other is "X" or "Y." The mind finds it very challenging to be tranquil with not being anything before being something.

The possible reason why we don't see the emptiness at our center is because that center is God. We are afraid to look at it because deep down we know death is there too. That center is the source of all that we are, and without it there's no motion. As of now, being close to such a center is not sustainable, but it is possible to come and go with relatively high frequency. Life is marvelous when it's lived near the center. Such a place is a fountain of creativity, knowledge, and joy. We sacrificed freedom for the sake of application. As incredible as it seems, that's what our lives have become. God, space, observation, motion, the present, etc., we can't measure these immensities of reality, and yet these are what give birth to the quality of every relationship in the universe. Peace, gratitude, joy, beauty, etc., these are all *unprogrammable features of the human condition.*

Society teaches us from a very young age the value of specialized knowledge, and in doing so we are giving up truth in the name of academic disciplines and the functioning of our socio-economic systems. The real job of institutional bodies is to govern and regulate, not to offer solutions. Let's not get it wrong though, governance aids in the addressing of solutions, but it does nothing to create them. I'm not talking about revolt or anarchy in regards to what keeps the actual human order. I'm just saying that we are trading diamonds for mirrors. Security is not granted by governance, but instead it is granted by order. The problem is that we don't really know what order is. I have the strong conviction that order and security – in actuality – are the same.

Concentration of knowledge leads to specific positions in society, but attention to the whole of reality brings joy and great relationship between us. Concentration is competition and advancement, and that is perfectly fine for innovation and achieving goals, but it leads nowhere in understanding life. Collaboration disarms the need for control because collaboration is born out of attention. In business, which propels a psychological occupation, there can't be attention. In business there is concentration, but not attention, and concentration inevitably fuels control. In fact, in order to concentrate one has to control oneself.

Let's look at the issue from another perspective. To observe is to pay attention, so whoever created the word attention saw that it must imply space as well.

The word *"attention"* comes from the Latin *"attentio,"* and it is composed by the prefix *"ad-,"* which means "towards, at," and the Latin word *"tendere,"* which means "stretch." Therefore, *"attention"* literally translates *"to stretch towards."* To stretch is to extend or expand. To expand is to reach out by means of increasing the space between the parts. However, unlike extension, which is also to expand but by splitting from the rest outwardly, attention doesn't fragment. Meaning, attention is to reach out without losing the whole integrity. Thus, to pay attention to reality, or one's life, is to be filled with space. Inwardly, it means the reaching of that space.

In contrast, the word "concentration" means the opposite of attention. *"Concentration"* is formed by the combination of the Latin prefix *"con-,"* which mean *"with, together,"* and the Latin word *"centrum,"* which means *"center."* By straight definition, to concentrate is to eliminate all space between the parts, so as to bring it all to a center. Therefore, concentration is to fill a center, instead of emptying it. A center that is filled with the weight of the self can't possibly create new realities. Since concentration is exclusion for the sake of focusing on one thing, for the observer it is conflictive in nature. It is then that to pay attention is to be receptive by expansion, and concentration is to narrow perception by rejection.

Our lives are in conflict because we live in concentration. Time gives us strength. Time is force. Time has built layer by layer, year after year, the society we live in now. We concentrate our strengths by living in groups. We created the family, then the cities and the countries we belong to. One inquires, what is the big issue about concentrating our way of living? Well, the problem lies in identifying according to a psychological construct. In our current lives, to concentrate the way we relate, we inevitably have had to identify ourselves with that which is creating the modern human momentum. Language and technology give us a better quality of life, but when we identify as "this or that" through them, it generates conflicts in our relationships.

Religions have tried to solve the problem by giving it a mystic angle. However, all religions unavoidably divide us because they place society's culture at the center of the several traits that characterize their "ideal" human, and with which its followers must identify. Religion's artifices are many images and metaphors in language, but that is just a concentration of symbols. Whatever methodology, which is the artificial achieved by technique, will unavoidably lead to more of the same. Religions "teach" compassion, but compassion can't be taught. Either one sees one is dying, or one is never going to see the human sorrow. If one doesn't see the sorrow in oneself, it is impossible to see it in another, and that requires a tremendous amount of attention. In other words, it is useless to concentrate mentally or physically – individually or collectively – in order to understand death, but it is possible to see truth in death by paying attention to the whole of life.

An important implication of eliminating the psychological framework of progression in thought, is that we'll immediately realize that psychological change is never gradual. Unlike physical change, which is a mechanical transformation, psychologically we simply are "xyz" or we just aren't. To absolutely stop and face time as it actually is, disarms the current structure of thought that time has conditioned. In other words, to change gradually gets you stuck in the same psychological situation because all progression always ends in the same way. An end always ends as the last thing, and that is what a purpose is. However, changing under the idea of time (i.e., gradually) always leads you to see an even further end from the one you started with at the beginning. Remember, time seeks to preserve, to keep on going in continuity, and psychologically that gets you in a never ending cycle of conflict. Meaning, to seek under an idealistic purpose will put you in a mental running wheel. In other words, any psychological purpose makes you a different version of the same thing.

The furthest of which is this unattainable edge that no knowledge can touch. The whole thing becomes frustrating for the observer. Physical goals are perfectly sane, but psychological ends are just illusions. A common conflict, which arises in trying to explain everything I'm putting forth, is that the listener's very first reaction usually is, "how's so?" or, "show me." That specific statement is application, and that is a blockage from time. We need fewer ideas in application to human relationships. We would rather not see it either because we lack a sincere intention. We lack creativity and energy, we run from our centers, and that's why we prefer hope.

In life, everything has a cycle. It is time to explore whether we can end this era's cycle to come back to pay attention to what really matters. All we do – the food we produce, the houses, the temples, the books – everything is made by a human for a human. One might say, "it was a robot that built it," but we built the robots. Alternatively, "the food is for the animals, not for humans," is also a deceit because the animal is either food itself, or a pet, or it has some sort of application and utility to a human. All we do, every single thing, is by us for us. The question is then, why do we give authority to our robots, our bombs, our words, or our Gods? We carry more power than a nuclear bomb. The problem has never been our artifacts, or how much more sophisticated in performance they are than us, but the authority we grant to them. The danger is not the nuclear weapon, but that we launch them. As powerful as nuclear weapons are, we are beyond their reach because we have an even greater power. As destructive as an atomic bomb is, it has no defense against us disarming it.

People die, but ideas survive. In conceding the sundial authority over our relationships we committed the most incredible mistake in history, which is the authority of progression over our social order. The idea of time, as it's currently applied, is like a tyrant from which we must seek freedom. I think that mistake is part of a conscious process, which in its realization will lead to higher orders of awareness in relationship to the whole of existence. Still, as of now the way things are, since we granted authority to our ideas, we started deviating from our purpose. There's nothing wrong in the idea of going to planet Mars, for example. However, will that solve our sorrow? The answer is no. The instant the first "Martian" is born, time on planet Mars will begin, and with it the continuity of all the nonsense we deal with here on Earth.

Our purpose is met through art. God is an artist, and that is the reason why men from the past say he created us in his image. It is not that we look like him, but we are his abstraction. It must be so, because as an abstraction we are. Out of that, the immediate possibility is energy, and energy in humans manifests as passion. In that passion lies all the change we could need.

Every once in a while, a mutant is born. I'm not talking about getting a third arm, or an extra sense, but a much deeper level of understanding of the fabric of us and reality. Throughout the ages, men with extraordinary capacity have shaped the course of humanity with unprecedented consequences. The extent of the impact of their mark is the reflection of how passionately these humans lived their lives. We ourselves are mutants of the human past. Nature produces changes in the raw materials of life out of deep levels of observation of the organism's condition. The question is, can we drive those mutations ourselves? That's what we want, right? If we do it purposely, we know that's the deceit of time. If we have an end in mind, then it is another idea. It doesn't mean "the mutation" won't take place. It might happen, or it might not. The issue is, when the idea is already out there, others will always find a way to exploit such direction towards "the change" to exploit the despair of the rest.

We need to see technology as an ally. The more time (as in the present) we have, the more attention we can bring to our lives. The troubled man can't change because he's trapped dealing with such problems – in what he thinks the solutions to them are, and in the pursuit of such solutions. He would have more immediate situations to attend to than taking on the challenge of attempting to solve the "unsolvable." What is ironic is that the whole of his activity is the result of his condition in the first place. His troubles are an issue of humanity. His cause is his doing, and it is the same cause of all mankind.

We have the idea that God created this world for us, but what is one to do in it? There's no such thing as the perfect answer. It's all about the right question. The right question sets the right quest. Humanity's purpose is a quest. Death is the result and meaning of that quest. Again, we need to stop thinking we have the solutions, because we don't (at all), and we need to start asking the corresponding questions without focusing so much on how different the answers are. *There's great art to be made in the right questioning of life, and in that lies the immensity of passion and love.*

_____

Ultimately, to observe is to love;
its function is to bring about motion.
To observe is to die before time.
Death is the unknown that doesn't split from space;
it is the wholeness of the reality of man.
Space is an unprogrammable continuum,
and we call it, "The quest of man."
To see the quest is to quest,
and that's the means to our end.

About the Author

Walter Mehrer is an economist and entrepreneur, a graduate from the University of Miami with special interest in the arts and philosophy. When it comes to the superficial issues of day-by-day living, he approaches matters as an economist and businessman. When it comes to human relationships and co-existence, he examines these phenomena as a philosopher whose passion is in the essence of life.

Walter M. was born in 1987. He currently lives in Miami, FL with his wife and children, where he continues to work on figuring out what it means to live a virtuous life.